DEUTSCHES
AUSWANDERER
HAUS®

off into the world

DAS BUCH ZUM DEUTSCHEN AUSWANDERERHAUS

THE GERMAN EMIGRATION CENTER BOOK

edition
DAH

European Museum of the Year Award 2007

Am 5. Mai 2007 erhielt das Deutsche Auswandererhaus in Alicante, Spanien, den bedeutendsten Preis der europäischen Museumslandschaft, den „European Museum of the Year Award".

Die von Henry Moore geschaffene Bronzeskulptur ging damit erstmals wieder seit 15 Jahren an ein deutsches Museum. Das Deutsche Auswandererhaus reiht sich ein in die Liste illustrer Preisträger wie beispielsweise das Victoria and Albert Museum in London und das Guggenheim Museum Bilbao.

Das Europäische Museumsforum zeichnet unter Federführung des Europarates seit seiner Gründung 1977 herausragende neue Projekte und Ideen auf dem Museumsgebiet in Europa aus. Einmal jährlich organisiert das Museumsforum unter dem Patronat von Königin Fabiola von Belgien den „European Museum of the Year Award", an dem sich neue oder umgebaute Museen beteiligen können. 50 Museen hatten sich für den Wettbewerb 2007 beworben.

Die emotionale Vermittlung von Geschichte über Inszenierungen, die dem Theater entlehnt sind, und die wissenschaftliche Aufbereitung des Themas waren ausschlaggebend für die Entscheidung der Juroren. Architektur, Konzept und Ausstellungsgestaltung des Deutschen Auswandererhauses stammen vom Studio Andreas Heller, Hamburg.

Seit seiner Eröffnung am 8. August 2005 begrüßte das Deutsche Auswandererhaus über 950.000 Besucher (Stand Oktober 2009) aus dem In- und Ausland.

The German Emigration Center was awarded the most coveted prize in the European museum landscape, the *European Museum of the Year Award*, at Alicante, Spain on 5 May 2007.

For the first time in 15 years, a German museum has once again won the award, a bronze sculpture by Henry Moore. The German Emigration Center now ranks among other illustrious prize-winners, among them the Victoria and Albert Museum in London and the Guggenheim Museum Bilbao.

Since its establishment in 1977, the European Museum Forum, operating under the auspices of the Council of Europe, has awarded outstanding projects and ideas in museums throughout Europe. Once a year, the European Museum Forum holds the *European Museum of the Year Award* under the patronage of Her Majesty Queen Fabiola of Belgium. Candidates for the award nomination are newly opened or restored museums. Fifty museums entered the 2007 award contest.

The emotional history using theater-based communication techniques and the approach used in treating this scientific topic were decisive factors for the jury. Architecture, concept and exhibition design were all carried out by Studio Andreas Heller, Hamburg.

Since its opening in August 2005, more than 950,000 visitors from Germany and abroad had visited and toured the German Emigration Center by October 2009.

EDITORIAL

Liebe Leserinnen, liebe Leser,

Lebensgeschichten voller Tragik oder strotzend vor Erfolg, geistreiches Feuilleton und reine Statistik, moderne Architektur und Inszenierungen, die dem Theater entlehnt sind, Originale und Rekonstruktionen ergänzen sich zur Gesamtkomposition des Deutschen Auswandererhauses.
Diese Vielfältigkeit spiegelt sich auch in diesem Buch wider. Es ist kein reiner Ausstellungskatalog, sondern auch ein lebendiges Geschichtsbuch mit reichhaltigen Informationen und einzigartigen Geschichten. Dieser zweiten Auflage haben wir drei Kapitel hinzugefügt: „Auswandern nach Argentinien", „Orte + Biographien: Die Sonderausstellungsthemen 2006–2009" und „Die Sammlung". Auch das Glossar wurde überarbeitet und ergänzt.
Ich wünsche allen Lesern die Anregung und Freude bei der Lektüre, die wir jeden Tag im Deutschen Auswandererhaus erfahren und freue mich, Sie (wieder) in Bremerhaven begrüßen zu dürfen.

Dear Reader,

Stories of lives touched by soft tragedy or gung-ho levity, refined wit or pure statistics; modern architecture and present-day productions borrowed from the stage, as well as originals and copies complement one another to create the overall composition which is the German Emigration Center.
The diversity is also reflected in this book which is far from merely being an exhibition catalogue but rather a vivid book combining in-depth information and one-of-a-kind stories. Three chapters have been added to the second edition: "Emigration to Argentina," "Sites + Biographies: Special Exhibition Themes 2006–2009" and "The Collection." Additions have also been made to the glossary.
I hope the readers of this book will be filled with the same excitement and joy we at the German Emigration Center experience everyday. I look forward to seeing you (again) in Bremerhaven.

Dr. Simone Eick
Direktorin / Director

Bremerhaven, Oktober / October 2009

INHALT / CONTENTS

VORWORT / PREFACE

Das Deutsche Auswandererhaus steht an einem der bedeutendsten historischen Erinnerungsorte des Wanderungsgeschehens: Rund die Hälfte der Massenauswanderung des 19. Jahrhunderts verließ Deutschland über Bremerhaven. In der Migrationsgeschichte war der deutsche Weg vom frühen 19. bis zum späten 20. Jahrhundert bestimmt durch den Wandel vom Auswanderungsland zum Einwanderungsland. Seither nimmt die Auswanderung wieder zu. Deutschland steht mit abnehmender Zuwanderung und zunehmender Auswanderung heute in der Mitte zwischen Ein- und Auswanderungsland. Im Grunde kehrt das Land damit in seine Geschichte zurück, denn es war oft Ein- und Auswanderungsland zugleich.
Die Kehrseite von Auswanderung ist Einwanderung, diejenige von Ausgliederung in der Alten ist die Eingliederung in die Neue Welt. Wer die aktuellen Fragen von Auswanderung und Rückwanderung, aber auch von Einwanderung und Integration und die damit verbundenen Probleme der Gegenwart und absehbaren Zukunft verstehen oder gestalten will, tut deshalb gut daran, historische Grunderfahrungen einzubeziehen. Die Geschichte bietet keine Patentrezepte für aktuelle Probleme, aber historische Grunderfahrungen als Orientierungshilfen für das Verständnis der Gegenwart und die Gestaltung der Zukunft.
Diesen Fundus an Erfahrungs- und Erlebniswelten auf eindringliche Weise zu erschließen, hat sich das Deutsche Auswandererhaus als Museum neuen Typs zur Aufgabe gemacht. Es leistet damit in Sachen Migration und Integration einen wichtigen Brückenschlag zwischen Geschichte und Gegenwart.

The site of the German Emigration Center is one of the most important memorial sites in the history of migration: almost half of the mass emigration wave during the 19th century departed from Germany via Bremerhaven. In the history of migration, the German approach from the time of the early 19 century through the late 20th century was defined by its transition from a country of emigration to a country of immigration. Since that time, however, emigration has been on the rise again. Today, Germany stands somewhere between declining immigration and rising emigration figures. Basically, the country is returning to its own historical roots, as it was often a place of immigration and emigration in the past.
The opposite of emigration is immigration, and the opposite of exclusion from the Old is inclusion in the New World. For those wanting to understand and shape the current issues of emigration and re-migration, but also of immigration and integration together with the related present problems and those of the foreseeable future it is highly advisable to involve fundamental historical experience. History does not offer a patent remedy for current problems, but fundamental historical experience does act as a guideline to understanding the present and shaping the future.
The German Emigration Center is a new type of museum committed to unlocking this rich source of knowledge and experience in a vivid and poignant manner, thereby connecting the topics of migration and integration with history, past and present.

Prof. Dr. Klaus J. Bade
Vorsitzender des Sachverständigenrates deutscher Stiftungen für Integration und Migration
Chairman of the Advisory Board of the German Foundations for Integration and Migration

Berlin, Oktober / October 2009

IN DIE NEUE WELT / OFF INTO THE NEW WORLD

7

IN DIE NEUE WELT
Auswanderung und Flucht aus Deutschland in den letzten zwei Jahrhunderten

OFF INTO THE NEW WORLD
Emigration and Escape from Germany during the Last Two Centuries

SIMONE EICK

Bremerhaven, im Jahr 1929

An der Columbuskaje: Der Passagierdampfer „Bremen" steht kurz vor der Abfahrt. Bunte Luftschlangen wehen im Wind: Das eine Ende halten an der Reling lehnende Auswanderer, das andere Ende die auf der Kaje stehenden Verwandten und Freunde. Sobald das Schiff losfährt, werden sich die Papierschlangen straffen und irgendwann reißen. Lebewohl. Weiße Taschentücher flattern im Wind. So manche haben einen Knoten im Zipfel: Vergiss mich nicht. Eine Kapelle spielt: „Muss i denn, muss i denn, zum Städtele hinaus..." Zeremonien des Abschieds. Etwas, an das man sich halten kann in diesem Augenblick voller Wehmut, Angst und Hoffnung. Da war er nun: Der Augenblick, nach dem man sich so sehr gesehnt hatte. Der Beginn des Traumes vom Leben in der Neuen Welt.

Bremerhaven, in 1929

The Columbus wharf. The passenger steamship *Bremen* is ready for departure. Colorful streamers are blowing in the wind, one end held by emigrant passengers leaning against the railing, the other end held by family and friends standing on the wharf waving their loved ones off. As soon as the ship casts off, the streamers will tighten and eventually rip. Good-bye, farewell. White handkerchiefs, some with knots tied in them, fluttering in the breeze, reminding those on board not to forget those back home. And a band playing the well-known tune "Muss I denn, muss I denn, zum Städtele hinaus..."

The farewell ceremony. Something to hold onto during this wistful, fearful moment full of hope and melancholy. Suddenly, it had arrived, the moment those leaving had so longed for. The beginning of their dream of a new life in the New World.

Sammlung Deutsches Auswandererhaus / Collection German Emigration Center

Die „Europa" beim Ablegen von der Columbuskaje in Bremerhaven, um 1930.

The Columbus wharf. The *Europa* sets sail for America, about 1930.

Ellis Island Immigration Museum

Die Neue Welt, das waren für Auswanderungswillige des 19. und 20. Jahrhunderts vor allem die Vereinigten Staaten von Amerika, Kanada, aber auch südamerikanische Staaten wie Brasilien und Argentinien sowie der fünfte Kontinent, Australien. Allein zwischen 1821 und 1914 wanderten 44 Millionen Europäer in die Neue Welt aus, davon 5,5 Millionen Deutsche. Heute gibt es mindestens 40 Millionen US-Amerikaner, die deutsche Vorfahren haben, manche Angaben gehen sogar von 50 Millionen aus. In Argentinien leben eine Million Menschen mit deutschen Wurzeln, in Kanada 2,7 Millionen, in Brasilien fünf Millionen und in Australien etwa 800.000.

The New World—for those eager to emigrate during the nineteenth and twentieth centuries that invariably meant the United States of America and Canada, but also the South American countries of Brazil and Argentina, and the fifth continent, Australia. Forty-four million Europeans emigrated to the New World between 1821 and 1914 alone, of which 5.5 million were German. No less than 40 million U.S. citizens today are of German extraction, some estimates even venture as high as 50 million. One million inhabitants of German descent live in Argentina, 2.7 million in Canada, five million in Brazil and an estimated 800,000 in Australia.

ullstein bild

Häuptling Crazy Horse in der legendären Schlacht vom Little Bighorn am 25.06.1876. Das Bild stammt aus dieser Zeit von einem Oglala Sioux Indianer aus dem Pine-Ridge-Reservat.
Chief Crazy Horse in the legendary Battle of Little Bighorn on 25 June 1876. The picture dates back to that time and was drawn by an Oglala Sioux Indian at the Pine Ridge Reservation.

Warum verließen ihre Vorfahren Deutschland? Und wie war diese Massenauswanderung möglich? In der heutigen Zeit der Einwanderungsbeschränkungen erscheinen ihre Wanderungsmöglichkeiten paradiesisch – aber auch sie hatten

What caused their ancestors to leave Germany? How was a mass emigration of this dimension even possible? In today's world of immigration restrictions the possibilities of onetime emigrants seem like heaven on earth, yet there was a

ihren Preis: die Vertreibung und Vernichtung der Mehrheit der ursprünglichen Bevölkerung.

Die ersten Europäer in der Neuen Welt gehörten den großen Seefahrernationen an: Briten, Portugiesen, Spanier und Niederländer. Während Portugiesen und Spanier zunächst Südamerika besetzten, eroberten die Briten und Franzosen Nordamerika; auch Australien wurde britisch. Die Kolonialherren wüteten in der Neuen Welt: Die ursprüngliche Bevölkerung wurde ermordet oder versklavt, Reichtümer hochzivilisierter Gesellschaften, wie die der Inka und Maya in Mittel- und Südamerika, wurden geraubt. Hatten beispielsweise in Mexiko um 1500 noch 25 Millionen Menschen gelebt, gab es um 1560, nach 60 Jahren spanischer Herrschaft, nur noch drei Millionen. Als die ersten größeren Gruppen deutscher Siedler Anfang des 19. Jahrhunderts nach Brasilien und Argentinien kamen, waren die ursprünglichen Kulturen bereits zerstört. Die Vertreibung und Ausrottung der Ureinwohner auf dem Gebiet der USA hatten ihren Höhepunkt im 19. Jahrhundert und waren auch eine Folge der europäischen Masseneinwanderung. Auch die eingewanderten deutschen Bauern errichteten ihre Farmen auf ehemaligen indianischen Gebieten.

Gerade die deutschen Kleinbauern waren auf der Suche nach freiem Land in die USA gekommen, denn in Deutschland herrschte seit Ende des 18. Jahrhunderts akuter Landmangel. War das Land nach dem Dreißigjährigen Krieg (1618–1648) noch stark entvölkert, kam es innerhalb von 150 Jahren durch das Erbteilungsgesetz zu Landmangel. Verstärkt wurde der Effekt im 19. Jahrhundert noch durch das seit dem Ende des 18. Jahrhunderts herrschende Bevölkerungswachstum. 75 Prozent der Bauern besaßen Mitte des 19. Jahrhunderts nicht ausreichend Land, um davon leben zu können. Sie waren auf einen Nebenerwerb angewiesen: Durch die stetig wachsende Bevölkerung kämpften immer mehr Menschen um solch einen Arbeitsplatz, gleichzeitig wurden traditionelle Berufe, die sich als Nebenerwerb eigneten, durch die Industrialisierung überflüssig. So verschlang

high price to pay. The men, women and children, all originally from Germany, who left the country in hordes at the time, were to a very great extent the victims of persecution or extermination or both.

The first Europeans to set foot in the New World came from seafaring nations—Great Britain, Portugal, Spain and the Netherlands. Whereas the Portuguese and Spanish first occupied and settled in South America, the British and French conquered and colonized North America; Australia, too, became a British possession. The colonial rulers wreaked havoc on the New World, slaying or enslaving the natives, and robbing the advanced Inca and Maya civilizations in Central and South America of their treasures. To think that Mexico, for example, numbering 25 million inhabitants in 1500, had dropped to a mere three million by 1560 after 60 years under Spanish rule, is rather hard to fathom. By the time the first large groups of German settlers arrived in Brazil and Argentina in the nineteenth century, the indigenous Indian population had already been wiped out. The persecution and extermination of Native Americans, which peaked in the nineteenth century, was none other than the direct result of mass European immigration to the United States. A large number of German farmers, in particular, set up farms on land once inhabited by Indians.

Particularly the German farmers who immigrated to America were in search of farming land. Whereas after the Thirty Years' War (1618–1648) Germany was extremely sparsely populated, the Estate Distribution Law changed conditions considerably over the ensuing 150 years, creating an acute shortage of land. By the beginning of the nineteenth century the effects were compounded by the population growth which had set in with the outgoing eighteenth century. By the mid-nineteenth century, 75 percent of the farmers depended on side jobs as they were unable to make a living for themselves and their families off the land they owned. Not only were a growing number of people seeking work due to the steady population increase, but jobs were invariably becoming scarce or obsolete as industrialization spread and new

Sammlung Deutsches Auswandererhaus / Collection German Emigration Center

Handbücher informierten Auswanderungswillige über Reisevorbereitungen, Lebensbedingungen und Geographie der Neuen Welt: „Der Führer nach Amerika", 1882; „Taschenbuch über die Vereinigten Staaten", 1923; „Katechismus der Auswanderung", 1881. / Those seriously considering emigration consulted manuals such as these for information on travel preparation, the economy and geography of the New World: *Der Führer nach Amerika* (The Guide to America), 1882; *Taschenbuch über die Vereinigten Staaten* (Pocketbook on the United States), 1923; *Katechismus der Auswanderung* (The Catechism of Emigration), 1881.

beispielsweise die rasant aufsteigende Textilindustrie nach und nach ganze Berufszweige: Leinenweber, Garnspinner, Schneider, Näherinnen und Stickerinnen. Die Spirale der Armut drehte sich für den unteren deutschen Mittelstand zwischen 1800 und 1850 immer schneller. Die Industrialisierung war in Deutschland zu diesem Zeitpunkt noch nicht so weit fortgeschritten, dass neue Berufszweige den von Armut bedrohten Menschen einen Ausweg geboten hätten. Typische deutsche Auswanderer Mitte des 19. Jahrhunderts waren Kleinbauern mit ihren Familien. Hinzu kamen Tagelöhner und Dienstmägde vom Lande und aus den Städten, die ebenfalls aufgrund des Bevölkerungswachstums von Arbeitslosigkeit bedroht waren. Die deutschen Auswanderer Mitte des 19. Jahrhunderts suchten Arbeit und freies Land. Die besten Chancen darauf hatten sie in den Vereinigten Staaten von Amerika. Der Rest der Neuen Welt bot schlechtere klimatische Bedingungen, weniger Jobs und eine größere Unsicherheit. Einige wagten es trotzdem nach Brasilien, Argentinien, Kanada und Australien auszuwandern.

Anders als in den USA gab es in Südamerika staatlich organisierte Kolonisationsprojekte, in denen den Siedlern freies Land, Steuerfreiheit und Befreiung vom Militärdienst zugesagt wurden. Das war auch bitter nötig, denn die Siedlungsbedingungen in weiten Teilen Brasiliens und Argentiniens waren extrem hart. Angesprochen wurden die Auswan-

jobs were increasingly difficult to come by. Gradually, entire trades and crafts were swallowed up by newly flourishing industries. The textile industry for one did away with the linen weaving, spinning, tailor's, dressmaking and embroidery trades. The lower middle classes in Germany between 1800 and 1850 were caught up in a downward spiral of rapidly growing poverty. At that time, industrialization in Germany was not sufficiently advanced to offer people whose work in certain trades was threatened by redundancy, and hence poverty, new opportunities in emerging industries. Thus German emigrants during the mid-eighteenth century were typically peasants, their families working as day laborers, maids and farm girls who, as a result of the rising population figures, were confronted with joblessness and little hope for anything but a bleak future. Hence, eighteenth-century German emigrants were in dire search of work and free land, both of which were available in great abundance in the United States of America. Nowhere else in the New World did the climatic conditions, the labor market and security

derungswilligen in Europa im Auftrag südamerikanischer Regierungen von Unternehmen und Reiseagenten, die wirtschaftlich von der Vermittlungszahl profitierten und oft skrupellos waren. Aber die Besiedlungsversuche unter für Europäer so ungewohnten klimatischen und geographischen Bedingungen endeten oft tragisch. Viele Menschen starben. Erfolgreich waren Siedlungsprojekte in Gebieten in der gemäßigten Zone, wie beispielsweise die deutsche Kolonie „São Leopoldo", gegründet 1824. Sie lag im Süden Brasiliens im Gebiet Rio Grande do Sul, wo bald weitere deutsche Siedlungen entstanden. Insgesamt wanderten zwischen 1820 und 1900 nur 101.800 Deutsche nach Brasilien und knapp 28.000 Deutsche nach Argentinien aus.

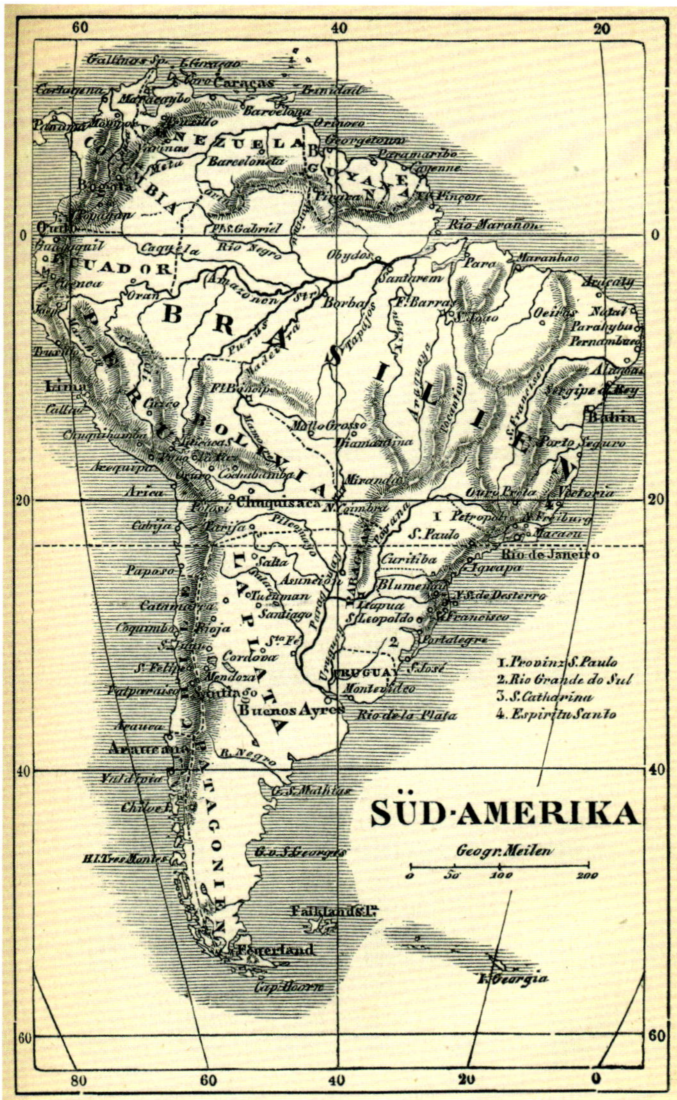

Sammlung Deutsches Auswandererhaus / Collection German Emigration Center

equal the standards offered in America. Nevertheless, many an emigrant ventured to Brazil, Argentina, Canada and Australia to try his luck.

In contrast to the United States, there were government-organized colonization projects in South America guaranteeing immigrant settlers open land, exemption from taxation and military service. All these benefits were sorely needed to attract settlers to the outback and extremely rough countryside prevailing in large areas of Brazil and Argentina. Companies and travel agents officially commissioned by South American governments approached potential emigrants in Europe, often profiting unscrupulously from the number of candidates they were able to acquire. For the Europeans, unaware and unfamiliar with the harsh climate and geographic conditions awaiting them in the new country, these attempts at land settlement invariably ended tragically. Countless immigrant settlers died, while those who settled in temperate zones, such as the German colony *São Leopoldo*, founded in 1824, were successful. This settlement in southern Brazil in the Rio Grande do Sul region was followed by various other German settlements. At the most, 101,800 Germans emigrated to Brazil and roughly 28,000 to Argentina between 1820 and 1900.

Australia too recruited new settlers during the nineteenth century, as virtually no European found the idea of forging a new life in a British colony inhabited by deported convicts terribly enticing. In contrast to an estimated 30,000 convicts who lived on the fifth continent in 1828, there were a mere 5,000 voluntary settlers from European countries. By 1840 the situation had improved from the standpoint of the immigrants with 50,000 deported convicts compared to a total of 65,000 voluntary settlers. About this time a large number of Germans chose to immigrate to Australia. All told, between 1847 and 1914 a total of 55,900 Germans left

Aus: Eduard Pelz: „Katechismus der Auswanderung", Leipzig, 1881. / From: Eduard Pelz: *Katechismus der Auswanderung* (The Catechism of Emigration), Leipzig, 1881.

Auch Australien musste im 19. Jahrhundert um Siedler werben – wenige Europäer wollten in der britischen Sträflingskolonie ihr Glück versuchen: 1828 gab es knapp 30.000 Sträflinge, aber nur 5.000 freiwillige europäische Siedler auf dem fünften Kontinent. 1840 sah die Lage aus der Sicht der Einwanderer schon angenehmer aus: 50.000 Deportierten standen 65.000 freiwillige Siedler gegenüber. Es ist auch der Zeitpunkt, zu dem eine größere Anzahl deutscher Einwanderer nach Australien kam; insgesamt gingen zwischen 1847 und 1914 55.900 Deutsche nach Australien. Deutsche Siedlungen entstanden im Barossa-Tal in South Australia und in Queensland. 1868 wurde die Deportation von Sträflingen nach Australien durch die britische Regierung abgeschafft.

Kanada litt bis weit ins 20. Jahrhundert unter der größeren Attraktivität der USA: Allein von 1861 bis 1971 wanderten 7.750.000 Menschen von Kanada aus, die meisten von ihnen gingen in die USA. Die erste größere Gruppe deutscher Siedler gelangte zwischen 1750 und 1753 nach Kanada: Das britische Königshaus warb für seine Kolonie 2.300 Auswanderer, von denen 1.500 deutschsprachig waren. Sie stammten aus der Schweiz, Norddeutschland und der Pfalz und siedelten sich in Neuschottland an. Von 1851 bis 1910 wanderten 89.100 Deutsche nach Kanada ein.

Erst im 20. Jahrhundert kam es zu stärkeren Auswanderungswellen von Deutschen nach Südamerika, Australien und Kanada. „Nach Amerika!", dieser Ruf, der im 19. Jahrhundert von Süddeutschland ausgehend immer schneller durch ganz Deutschland hallte, meinte vor allem die Vereinigten Staaten von Amerika. Briefe von erfolgreich eingewanderten Verwandten forderten die in Deutschland zurückgebliebenen Verwandten, Freunde und Bekannten auf, es doch ebenfalls im Land der unbegrenzten Möglichkeiten zu versuchen. So setzte vor allem in der zweiten Hälfte des 19. Jahrhunderts eine starke Kettenwanderung ein.

Am Anfang der deutschen Masseneinwanderung in die USA standen im 18. Jahrhundert Menschen auf der Suche nach

their homeland for Australia. German colonies emerged in the Barossa Valley in South Australia and in Queensland. Finally, in 1868, the British government abolished the deportation of convicts to Australia.

In terms of attracting immigrants Canada took a back seat to the United States well into the twentieth century. In fact, 7,750,000 residents emigrated from Canada between 1861 and 1971, the majority immigrating across the border to the United States. The first sizeable group of Germans to settle in Canada is recorded between 1750 and 1753. At the time, the British monarchy recruited 2,300 emigrants for its colony, of which 1,500 happened to be German-speaking from Switzerland, Northern Germany and the Palatinate, and settling in Nova Scotia. From 1851 to 1910, a total of 89,100 Germans immigrated to Canada.

It wasn't until the twentieth century that large waves of emigrants left Germany for South America, Australia and Canada. The words "To America!," so often heard in nineteenth-century Southern Germany, now echoed throughout the country, referring to the United States of America. Letters from German immigrants to the U.S. regaling relatives, friends and acquaintances back home with their newly found lives and success encouraged increasing numbers of Germans to try their luck in the land of endless opportunity as well, culminating in a wave of chain-reaction emigration during the latter half of the nineteenth century.

Two principal aspects influenced the onset of mass German immigration to the United States in the eighteenth century, the search for individual religious freedom and the desire for men, even entire families, to be hired or contracted by large plantation owners for a specified period as indentured servants.

The first all-German settlement in the U.S.A. was Germantown, Pennsylvania, founded in 1683 by 13 families from Krefeld under the leadership of Franz Daniel Pastorius, a Mennonite seeking religious freedom for his religious community in the U.S. The *Amish*, a strict Mennonite sect that

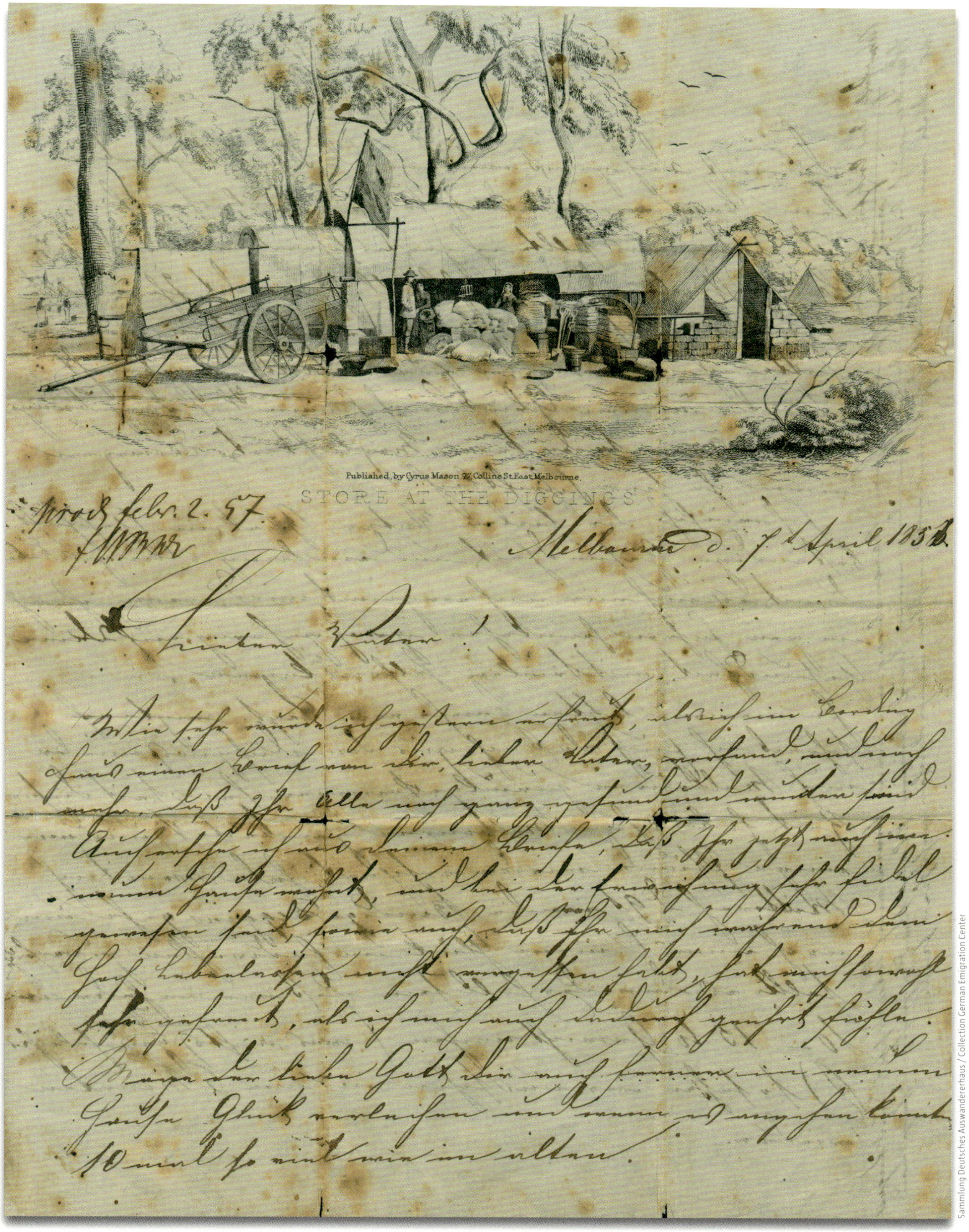

Brief aus Australien an die Familie in Deutschland, Melbourne, 1856. / Letter from Australia to the family in Germany, Melbourne, 1856.

Religionsfreiheit und die „indentured servants", Männer, aber auch ganze Familien, die ihre Arbeitskraft auf Zeit an amerikanische Großgrundbesitzer verkauften.
Die erste geschlossene deutsche Siedlung in den USA war Germantown in Pennsylvania. Gegründet wurde sie 1683 von 13 Krefelder Familien unter ihrem Anführer Franz Daniel Pastorius, einem Mennoniten, der in den USA mit seiner Gemeinde freie Religionsausübung suchte. Eine weitere deutsche Religionsgemeinschaft ließ sich Ende des 18. Jahrhunderts in Pennsylvania nieder: Die „Amische", eine Glaubensgemeinschaft, die ursprünglich in Süddeutschland beheimatet war, hatten sich 1693 aufgrund ihrer strengeren Lebensvorstellungen von den Mennoniten abgespalten. Um 1700 wanderten größere Gruppen von ihnen nach Nordamerika aus und ließen sich in Pennsylvania nieder. Die „amish people" leben auch heute noch in den USA als geschlossene religiöse Gemeinschaft, in der die meisten Mitglieder jeglichen Komfort ablehnen, keinen Strom und keine Autos nutzen und sich dem Militärdienst verweigern.
Eine Mehrheit deutscher Einwanderer in den USA stellten im 18. Jahrhundert die „indentured servants": In Deutschland mittellos lebend, ohne Geld für die Schiffspassage, verkauften sie ihre Arbeitskraft ebenso wie die ihrer Familienmitglieder für vier oder mehr Jahre an amerikanische Großgrundbesitzer. Diese bezahlten die Überfahrt und übernahmen Kost und Logis für die Dauer des Dienstverhältnisses. Am Ende erhielten die Arbeiter meist noch etwas Geld und ein eigenes Stück Land von ihrem Dienstherren. In die Selbstständigkeit entlassen, hatten sie die gleichen Rechte und Pflichten wie alle Bürger der britischen Kolonien in Nordamerika. Als 1776 nordamerikanische Kolonien ihre Unabhängigkeit von Großbritannien erklärten und sich Vereinigte Staaten von Amerika nannten, lebten etwa 300.000 Deutsche dort.

Napoleon hatte Europa zwischen 1792 und 1815 mit seinen Freiheitskriegen überzogen, aber er verbreitete auch die Ideen von „Freiheit, Gleichheit und Brüderlichkeit". Die Gedanken der Aufklärung, die zuvor nur Politiker

separated from the Mennonite community in 1693 and originally came from Southern Germany, were another German religious group to settle in Pennsylvania in the late eighteenth century. Large numbers of *Amish* immigrated to the U.S. around 1700, all settling in Pennsylvania. The *Amish* people continue to live today as a closed religious community. They are noted for their simplicity of life, rejecting virtually all comforts including electricity and automobiles, and refusing to do military service.
Indentured servants constituted the majority of German immigrants to the U.S. in the eighteenth century. These people, destitute in Germany, had no means of paying for their passage to America, hence selling themselves and their families as laborers to land owners in the United States for a period of four or more years. The land owners in turn paid their passage and provided the indentured servants living quarters and food for the tenure of their service. When the contracted period was over, most employers gave the laborers money and a piece of land to work. Thus released into a life of independence, these men and women had the same rights and duties as any citizen of the North American British colonies. An estimated 300,000 Germans lived in the United States of America at the time the colonies obtained their independence from Great Britain in 1776.

Although Napoleon had waged wars of liberation all over Europe from 1792 to 1815, he also disseminated the concept of "freedom, equality and brotherhood." The reasoning behind the intellectual movement of the Age of Enlightenment, until now the sole domain of thinkers, politicians and writers, suddenly became accessible to everyone. The politician and philosopher Friedrich Gentz speaks of the revolution in 1790 as "the first practical triumph of philosophy, the hope and consolation for many of the ills which previously weighed so heavily on mankind. Should this revolution abate, these very ills would be past remedy tenfold."[1] With the defeat of Napoleon in 1815, the governments of the German states largely revoked the reforms carried out in the regions formerly occupied by the French. Henceforth German farmers continued

Sammlung Deutsches Auswandererhaus / Collection German Emigration Center

Links: Weizenspeicher in Wichita, Sedgwick County, Kansas. Aus: Adolf Ott: „Der Führer nach Amerika", Basel, 1882. Rechts: Familie Breit vor ihrer Farm im brasilianischen Santa Cruz do Sul, um 1925. / Left: Grain silo in Wichita (Sedgwick County), Kansas. Taken from Adolf Ott: *Der Führer nach Amerika* (The Guide to America), Basle, 1882. Right: The Breit family outside their barn in Santa Cruz do Sul, Brazil, about 1925.

und Intellektuelle verfolgt hatten, berührten nun alle. Der Politiker und Philosoph Friedrich Gentz schrieb über die Revolution 1790: „Sie ist der erste praktische Triumph der Philosophie. (...) Sie ist die Hoffnung und der Trost für so viel alte Übel, unter denen die Menschheit seufzt. Sollte diese Revolution zurückgehen, so würden alle diese Übel zehnmal unheilbar." [1] Nachdem Napoleon 1815 besiegt war, nahmen die deutschen Regierungen Reformen, die in den zuvor französisch besetzten deutschen Gebieten eingeführt worden waren, wieder weitestgehend zurück. Die deutschen Bauern litten weiterhin unter ihren Abgabenlasten. Dort, wo sie abgelöst werden konnten, mussten die Bauern oft Schulden aufnehmen, um die Ablösung bezahlen zu können. Die Unfreiheit und die Nichtbeteiligung an der Politik blieben für alle Untertanen weiterhin bestehen. 1848 kam es zur Revolution, aber die demokratischen Kräfte in Deutschland scheiterten. Anführer der Revolution wurden steckbrieflich gesucht und flohen ins Ausland. Bekanntestes Beispiel ist Carl Schurz. Der Anführer des badischen Aufstandes flüchtete zunächst nach Frankreich, dann nach Großbritannien und schließlich in die USA. Dort ging er in die Politik. 1868 wurde er Senator des US-Bundesstaates Missouri und von 1877 bis 1881 „Secretary of the Interior". Zahlenmäßig

to suffer from the tax burdens and were frequently forced to borrow money in order to pay off tax debts. People continued to live in bondage and were excluded from politics. Finally in 1848 the people rose in revolt, but the forces of democracy did not prevail. The leaders of the revolution were on the wanted list and fled the country. Carl Schurz is a prominent example of that time. The leader of the Baden revolt first escaped to France, then to Great Britain, landing ultimately in the United States where he went into politics. In 1868 he was elected senator of Missouri and was Secretary of the Interior from 1877 to 1881. The percentage of 1848 revolutionaries who emigrated to the U.S. was small in numbers, but the failure of the 1848 revolution was for many final proof that Germany was not charting a course of change, hence creating additional motivation to seek a new way of life in the U.S.A.

Economic reasons were the driving force behind the majority of German emigrants to the United States in the nineteenth

war der Anteil der 1848er Revolutionäre an der deutschen Amerikaauswanderung gering, aber das Scheitern der Revolution war für viele Menschen der endgültige Beweis, dass sich in Deutschland wenig ändern würde. So stellte das Scheitern der demokratischen Bewegung 1848 für viele Menschen eine zusätzliche Motivation dar, in die demokratischen USA auszuwandern.

Bei der Mehrheit der Deutschen, die im 19. Jahrhundert in die USA auswanderten, überwogen wirtschaftliche Motive. Die Bauern lockte das freie Land oder zumindest die Möglichkeit, nach einigen Jahren als Lohnarbeiter eine Farm erwerben zu können. Um 1850 war die Gründung einer Farm eine einfache Angelegenheit: Nachdem sichergestellt war, dass auf dem gewünschten Stück Land kein anderer siedelte, steckte man es für sich ab und besaß damit einen „claim", einen Rechtsanspruch. Nach vier Jahren musste man für das Land bezahlen: 1 Acre (0,4 ha) kostete 1,25 Dollar. Viele begannen mit 40 Acres (16 Hektar), für die sie 50 Dollar zahlten. Kleinbauern, die in Deutschland unter fünf Hektar Land besessen hatten, konnten nach 15 Jahren harter Arbeit in den USA eine Farm besitzen, die 160 Acres, also 64 Hektar groß war. Solche Erfolgsgeschichten veranlassten in Deutschland gebliebene Verwandte und Freunde ebenfalls auszuwandern. Es entstanden zahlreiche deutsche Gemeinden, in denen es deutsche Schulen, Kirchen und Vereine gab und in denen deutsch gesprochen wurde. Gleichzeitig feierten die Bewohner amerikanische Feste wie „Halloween" oder den „Columbus Day" am 12. Oktober, an dem die Entdeckung Amerikas durch Christoph Columbus zelebriert wird. Es waren typische Deutsch-Amerikaner; sie gehörten zu den klassischen „Hyphen-Americans" (Bindestrich-Amerikanern).

Ende des 19. Jahrhunderts, als es in den von Deutschen bevorzugten Siedlungsgebieten wie dem Mittleren Westen, Texas und Kansas kaum noch freies Land gab, wurden Farmen teurer. So zogen viele Deutsche zunächst als Lohnarbeiter in boomende Städte wie New York oder Chicago. Chicago beispielsweise hatte 1830 erst 50 Einwohner, 1880

century. Peasants and farmers were attracted by the promise of land availability or at least the chance to buy farmland after earning wages for a number of years as a hired hand. Setting up a farm was an easy task in and around 1850. Once determined that a desired piece of land had not been staked out by anybody else, one was entitled to put a claim on it. Four years later, payment of the land was required: one acre (0.4 ha) cost one dollar and twenty-five cents. Most land claims started at 40 acres (16 ha), adding up to a total of fifty dollars. Small farmers who had owned a scant five hectares back home in Germany, now owned 160 acre (64 ha) farms after 15 years of hard work. It comes as no surprise that success stories of this type encouraged relatives and friends to follow in their fellow emigrants' footsteps. Various German communities came into being and with them German schools, churches and clubs. This did not prevent people from celebrating American holidays such as *Halloween* or *Columbus Day* (October 12, the day commemorating Christopher Columbus' discovery of America). They were typical German-Americans, so-called *hyphen-Americans*.

As by the late nineteenth century there was only very little unclaimed land left in the Middle West, Texas and Kansas, the regions most favored by Germans, farms went up in price. German immigrants began moving to major cities such as Chicago and New York where they took jobs as laborers. Chicago, for example, which in 1830 counted no more than a scant 50 inhabitants, had evolved into a bustling city of over one half million inhabitants, by 1880. After years of scrimping and saving, a large number of German immigrants was finally able to buy a farm.

During the nine-year period spanning 1880 to 1889, some 1,362,500 Germans emigrated, with 200,000 people leaving Germany in each of the two peak years 1881 and 1882 due to a severe economic crisis. The German Empire, booming economically for two years following its formation, suddenly collapsed. Businesses and companies went broke, unemployment soared. It wasn't until 1887 that the German

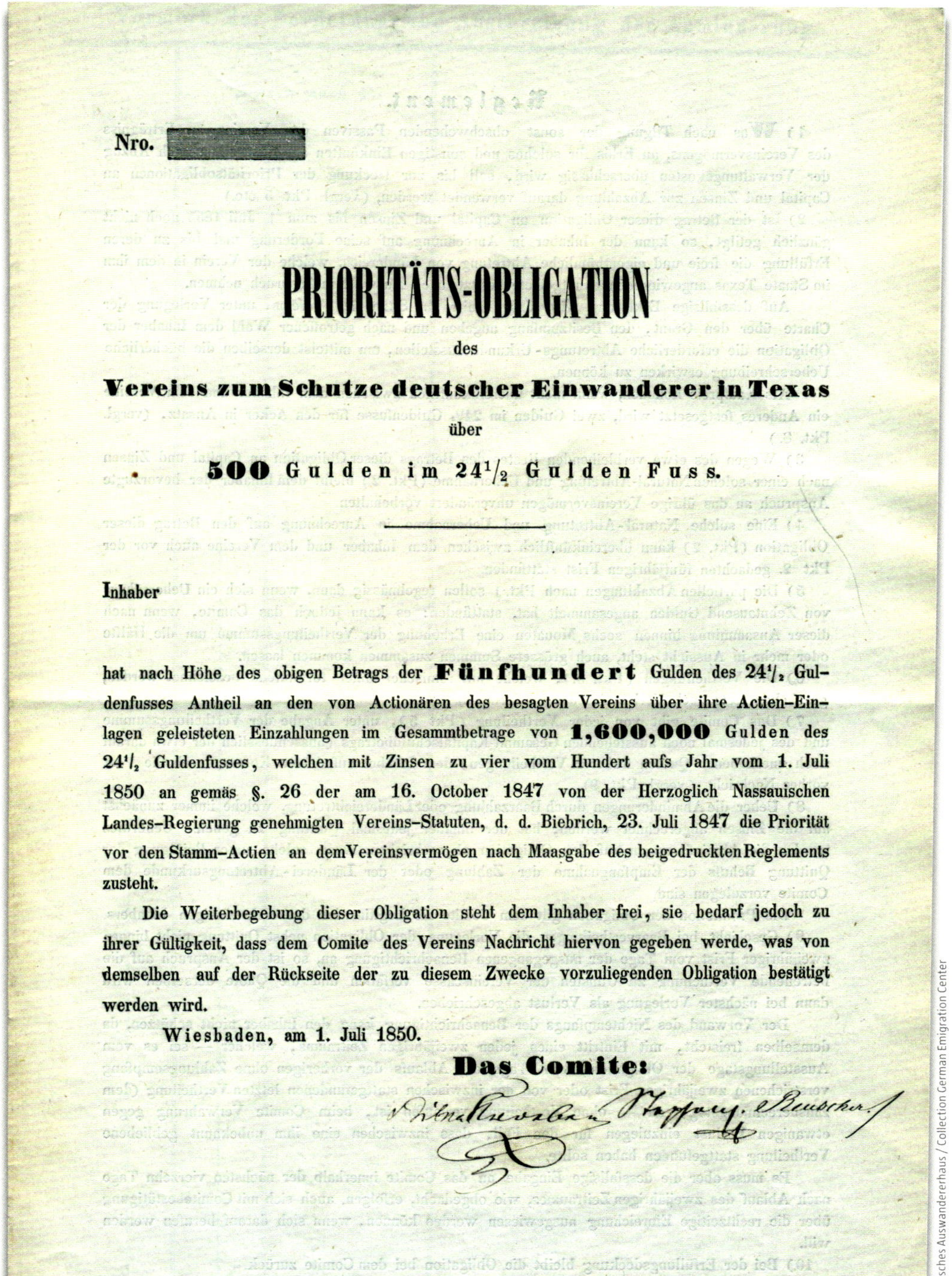

Nro. [redacted]

PRIORITÄTS-OBLIGATION

des

Vereins zum Schutze deutscher Einwanderer in Texas

über

500 Gulden im 24½ Gulden Fuss.

Inhaber

hat nach Höhe des obigen Betrags der **Fünfhundert** Gulden des 24½ Guldenfusses Antheil an den von Actionären des besagten Vereins über ihre Actien-Einlagen geleisteten Einzahlungen im Gesammtbetrage von **1,600,000** Gulden des 24½ Guldenfusses, welchen mit Zinsen zu vier vom Hundert aufs Jahr vom 1. Juli 1850 an gemäs §. 26 der am 16. October 1847 von der Herzoglich Nassauischen Landes-Regierung genehmigten Vereins-Statuten, d. d. Biebrich, 23. Juli 1847 die Priorität vor den Stamm-Actien an dem Vereinsvermögen nach Maasgabe des beigedruckten Reglements zusteht.

Die Weiterbegebung dieser Obligation steht dem Inhaber frei, sie bedarf jedoch zu ihrer Gültigkeit, dass dem Comite des Vereins Nachricht hiervon gegeben werde, was von demselben auf der Rückseite der zu diesem Zwecke vorzuliegenden Obligation bestätigt werden wird.

Wiesbaden, am 1. Juli 1850.

Das Comite:

Sammlung Deutsches Auswandererhaus / Collection German Emigration Center

Prioritäts-Obligation des „Vereins zum Schutze deutscher Einwanderer in Texas" über 500 Gulden im 24 ½ Gulden Fuß, Wiesbaden, 1850. Der Verein (1842–1848), auch „Mainzer Adelsverein" genannt, vermittelte zwischen 1844 und 1874 mehr als 7.300 deutsche Auswanderer nach Texas. Das Projekt mit dem Ziel der Gründung einer deutschen Kolonie in Texas endete für den Verein in einem finanziellen Debakel, versprochene große Landzuweisungen an Auswanderungswillige blieben aus.

Priority obligations from the *Verein zum Schutze deutscher Einwanderer in Texas* (Association for the Protection of German Immigrants to Texas) worth 500 guilders in 24 ½ guild feet, Wiesbaden, 1850. The registered association, also known as the *Mainzer Adelsverein* (Mainz Association of Nobility), acted as an agent for more than 7,300 German immigrants to Texas between 1844 and 1874. The project originally aimed at setting up a German colony in Texas, however, eventually defaulted and large land grants promised to German emigrants never materialized.

lebten dort bereits über eine halbe Million Menschen. Nach einigen Jahren des Sparens war es dann für viele deutsche Einwanderer möglich eine Farm zu erwerben.

Allein zwischen 1880 und 1889 wanderten 1.362.500 Deutsche aus. Höhepunkte waren die Jahre 1881 und 1882, in denen jeweils über 200.000 Menschen gingen. Ursache für diese starke Auswanderungsbewegung war eine schwere Wirtschaftskrise: Nachdem die deutsche Wirtschaft nach der Gründung des Deutschen Kaiserreiches 1871 für zwei Jahre geboomt hatte, brach sie danach umso stärker ein. Unternehmenspleiten und Arbeitslosigkeit waren die Folge. Erst ab 1887 erholte sich die deutsche Wirtschaft wieder dauerhaft und es begann in Deutschland eine Zeit der Vollbeschäftigung.
Anhand dieses Zeitraumes lassen sich klassische Muster von Auswanderungswellen aufzeigen, die sich in der Migrationsgeschichte wiederholen: Selten kommt es zu Massenauswanderungen zu Beginn einer Wirtschaftskrise. Einige Jahre lang hoffen die Menschen auf Verbesserung, auf einen Job, auf eine bessere Zukunft im Heimatland. Nach fünf wirtschaftlich schlechten Jahren beginnen die Auswandererzahlen zu steigen. Eine solche Situation ist auch im heutigen Deutschland zu beobachten: Infolge der Wirtschaftskrisen seit dem Jahr 2000 bestehen gleich bleibend hohe Auswandererzahlen um 150.000 pro Jahr. Das sind die höchsten Zahlen seit Bestehen der Bundesrepublik Deutschland. Aufgrund der besseren Arbeitsmarktsituation der europäischen Nachbarländer und der strikten Einwanderungsgesetze in den klassischen Einwanderungsländern wie USA, Kanada und Australien gingen die meisten deutschen Auswanderer 2000 bis 2008 in europäische Nachbarländer. Die Finanzkrise von 2008/2009 wird die Chancen deutscher Auswanderungswilliger im europäischen Ausland und in den USA Aufnahme zu finden, stark verringern. 2009 kommt es bereits zu ersten Rückwanderungen gescheiterter deutscher Auswanderer.

Wer im 19. und frühen 20. Jahrhundert den Plan zur Auswanderung gefasst hatte, kaufte bei einem Auswandereragenten

economy began to slowly and steadily recover, ushering in an era of full employment.
This period in time is a perfect example of how migratory movements occur. Seldom, if ever, does emigration result at the outset of an economic crisis. People are confident things will improve, they hope to find a job, a better future in their mother country. If an economy falters over a period of five years emigration figures tend to rise. We are witnessing the same situation in Germany today. As a result of the economic crises since 2000 the emigration figure is consistently high with approximately 150,000 German nationals emigrating every year. These figures are the highest since the foundation of the Federal Republic of Germany. Most have chosen neighboring European countries to emigrate to, as the job market is invariably better in those countries and immigration restrictions not as tight as in the classic immigration countries U.S.A., Canada and Australia. For Germans presently wishing to emigrate, the financial crisis of 2008/2009 will reduce chances of acceptance in other European countries or the U.S.A. By 2009, the first failed emigrants returned home to Germany.

When in the nineteenth and early twentieth centuries the decision to emigrate had been made, a passage was purchased through an emigration agent and the journey to the designated seaport began. While at first German emigrants headed for the seaports of Le Havre (France), Rotterdam (Netherlands) and Liverpool (England), the first German port of emigration was Bremerhaven, developing in the 1830s.

Hamburg was rather late in discovering the lucrative business of emigration. In fact, it wasn't until the 1840s that the city began to establish itself as a port of embarkation. In 1847, the *Hamburg-Amerikanische Packetfahrt-Actien-Gesellschaft* (Hapag) shipping line was formed, initially operating sailing ships, followed by regular steamship service between Hamburg and the United States in the 1880s. As of 1889, Hapag ships no longer sailed from Hamburg, but largely from the North Sea port of Cuxhaven. Altogether 5.5 million people

Sammlung Deutsches Auswandererhaus / Collection German Emigration Center

Auswanderer der III. Klasse besteigen an der Columbuskaje in Bremerhaven ein Schiff. Als Passagiere des Zwischendecks mussten sie ihr Gepäck selber tragen, um 1920.
Emigrants in steerage board the ship docked at the Columbus wharf in Bremerhaven, about 1920. Steerage passengers had to carry their own baggage on board.

eine Schiffspassage und machte sich auf den Weg an die Küste. Standen zunächst für deutsche Auswanderer vor allem das französische Le Havre, das niederländische Rotterdam und das britische Liverpool als Einschiffungshafen zur Verfügung, stellte ab den 1830er Jahren Bremerhaven den ersten deutschen Auswandererhafen. Bremerhaven und Hamburg wurden die größten deutschen Auswandererhäfen.

Hamburg entdeckte relativ spät das lukrative Geschäft mit den Auswanderern: Erst in den 1840er Jahren begann sich die Stadt als Einschiffungshafen zu etablieren. 1847 wurde die „Hamburg-Amerikanische Packetfahrt-Actien-Gesellschaft" (Hapag) gegründet, die zunächst mit Segelschiffen, ab den 1880er Jahren auch mit Dampfschiffen einen regelmäßigen Verkehr zwischen Hamburg und den USA einrichtete. Ab 1889 fuhren die Schiffe der Hapag größtenteils nicht mehr von Hamburg, sondern von Cuxhaven ab. Insgesamt reisten auf Schiffen unter Hamburger Flagge 5,5 Millionen Menschen: Leider liegen noch keine exakten Zahlen darüber

sailed to America on ships under the Hamburg flag. Unfortunately, exact figures as to the percentage of passengers who were emigrants, businessmen or tourists do not exist.

The mouth of the Weser River, December 1847

The sailing ship *Bremen* cast off from Bremerhaven an hour ago and has set sail for the North Sea. One hundred and sixty-nine passengers are on board, among them the Laufkoetter family. Auguste and Clemens Laufkoetter with their six children Emilie (11), Johann (9), Hermine (7), Louise (4), Fritz (3) and Pauline (1). The ship's destination is New Orleans. At worst, the crossing can take up to 15 weeks or longer. The Laufkoetters share a bunk measuring about 2.25 m in breadth and 1.70 m in length—a total of 3.8 sq. m. in space for the entire family to eat, sleep, live during the

vor, wie viele von diesen Passagieren Auswanderer und wie viele Geschäftsleute und Touristen waren.

Wesermündung, im Dezember des Jahres 1847

Das Segelschiff „Bremen" hat Bremerhaven vor einer Stunde verlassen und nimmt Kurs auf die Nordsee. An Bord befinden sich 169 Passagiere, unter ihnen auch die Familie Laufkötter. Auguste und Clemens Laufkötter mit ihren sechs Kindern Emilie (11), Johann (9), Hermine (7), Louise (4), Fritz (3) und Pauline (1). Ziel der Reise ist New Orleans; schlimmstenfalls dauert die Fahrt 15 Wochen oder noch länger. Die Familie Laufkötter teilt sich eine Koje, die etwa 2,25 m breit und

entire ocean crossing. The food is drab and unhealthy, the family's diet consists of zwieback, pulses, porridge, bacon and brackish water. In good weather conditions passengers are allowed to go up on deck once a day; in stormy conditions the hatch stays closed. Many of the passengers are seasick and fatal diseases, such as typhoid fever and dysentery, spread easily in the stale air between decks. Two to three percent of the passengers die on ships from Bremen in the nineteenth century, a low death rate by comparison to the English and Irish ships. The Laufkoetters are lucky. They arrive safe and sound in New Orleans on Feburary 11, 1848. Their trail is lost in the New World.

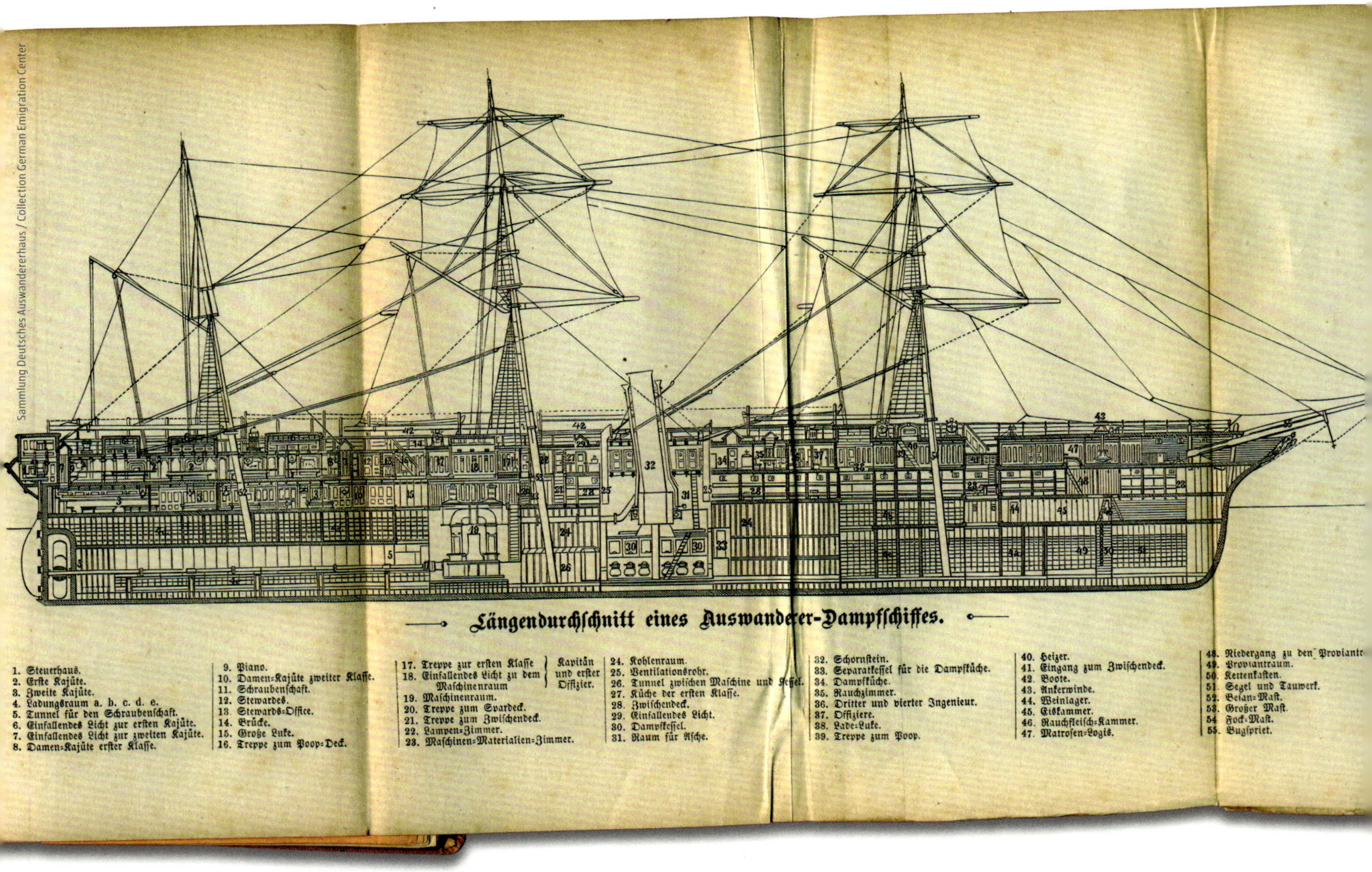

Sammlung Deutsches Auswandererhaus / Collection German Emigration Center

Längsschnitt eines Auswandererdampfschiffes. Aus: Eduard Pelz: „Katechismus der Auswanderung", Leipzig, 1881. Bis in die 1870er Jahre überquerten die meisten Auswanderer den Atlantik auf Segelschiffen. 18 Wochen konnte die Überfahrt dauern. Mit Einführung der Dampfschiffe verringerte sich die Reisedauer nach Amerika zunehmend auf acht bis 15 Tage. / Longitudinal section of a steamship carrying emigrants. Taken from Eduard Pelz: *Katechismus der Auswanderung* (The Catechism of Emigration), Leipzig, 1881. Up through 1870, the majority of emigrants made the long ocean journey to America on sailing ships with the crossing lasting up to 18 weeks. With the advent of the steamship the length of the journey dropped to eight, at the most 15 days.

1,70 m lang ist: 3,8 qm, auf denen sie schlafen, essen, leben muss – über Wochen. Das Essen ist eintönig und ungesund: Zwieback, Hülsenfrüchte, Getreidebrei, Speck und brackiges Wasser. Bei gutem Wetter können die Auswanderer einmal pro Tag an Deck, bei Sturm bleibt die Luke geschlossen. Die Seekrankheit plagt viele Menschen, lebensgefährliche Krankheiten wie Typhus und Ruhr verbreiten sich rasend schnell im engen Zwischendeck. Mitte des 19. Jahrhunderts sterben auf Bremer Schiffen zwei bis drei Prozent der Passagiere. Im Vergleich mit den englischen und irischen Schiffen ist das eine niedrige Sterbeziffer. Die Familie Laufkötter hat Glück: Sie kommt am 11. Februar 1848 heil in New Orleans an. Danach verliert sich ihre Spur in der Neuen Welt.

Bremerhaven wurde 1827 als Seehafen von der Hansestadt Bremen gegründet. Das erste Hafenbecken, heute der „Alte Hafen", wurde 1830 nach dreijähriger Bauzeit eröffnet. Ursprünglich als Handelshafen geplant, wurde Bremerhaven schnell zum Auswandererhafen. Die Bremer Kaufleute, deren Segelschiffe Waren wie Tabak, Baumwolle, Tee und Petroleum aus der Neuen Welt nach Europa brachten, konnten auf dem Hinweg mit der Auslastung der Schiffe durch den Transport von Auswanderern sehr gute Gewinne erzielen. Durch die Bremer „Verordnung wegen der Auswanderer mit hiesigen oder fremden Schiffen" von 1832 wird Bremerhaven zum modernen Auswandererhafen: Mindeststandards müssen auf den Schiffen, die unter Bremer Flagge fahren, eingehalten werden. Die Schiffe gelten so unter den Auswanderungswilligen als sicher. Als 1849 das Auswandererhaus, in dem bis zu 2.000 Auswanderer zu günstigen Preisen und unter guten hygienischen Bedingungen logieren können, in Bremerhaven eingerichtet wird, steigt die Stadt zum beliebtesten Auswandererhafen für Deutsche auf.
Als 1857 der „Norddeutsche Lloyd" gegründet wurde, gab es die erste regelmäßige Dampfschiffsverbindung zwischen Deutschland und den USA. Heimathafen des „Norddeutschen Lloyd" war Bremerhaven, die Schiffe fuhren unter Bremer Flagge. Die Reederei stieg Ende des 19. Jahrhunderts zur weltweit größten Passagierdampfschifffahrtsge-

Bremerhaven was established as a seaport by the Hanseatic city of Bremen in 1827, with the first harbor basin, the so-called *Alter Hafen*, or old port, opened after a three-year construction period in 1830. Originally planned as a port of trade, Bremerhaven quickly developed into a port of emigration. Bremen merchants whose ships transported goods from the New World such as tobacco, cotton, tea and mineral oil back to Europe, profited of course handsomely by transporting emigrant passengers from Europe to the New World when they would otherwise return empty. The Bremen Decree of 1832 actually contributed to making Bremerhaven a modern port of emigration by ensuring that minimal standards were maintained on all ships sailing under the Bremen flag. Among emigrants, the ships had a reputation of being safe. When the Emigration House, a boarding house of sorts offering reasonable room and board and good sanitary conditions with a capacity of up to 2,000, opened in Bremerhaven in 1849, the port town advanced to become the Germans' leading port of emigration.
Regular steamship service between Germany and the United States went into operation with the founding of *North German Lloyd* in 1857. The line's home port was Bremerhaven and ships sailed under the Bremen flag. By the end of the nineteenth century, the shipping line had grown to become the world's largest passenger steamship company with routes to North and South America, Asia and Australia. Millions of Germans and East Europeans emigrated to the New World on board ships operated by *North German Lloyd.*

A total of 7.2 million people emigrated to the New World by way of Bremerhaven between 1830 and 1974. Almost half this number—3.4 million—were from Eastern Europe and were primarily Polish, Russian, Czech, Slovak, Hungarian or Rumanian. The first major emigration wave from Eastern Europe set in during the 1880s and ended with World War I. The next major wave of emigrants arrived at this port of embarkation during the 1920s. East Europeans

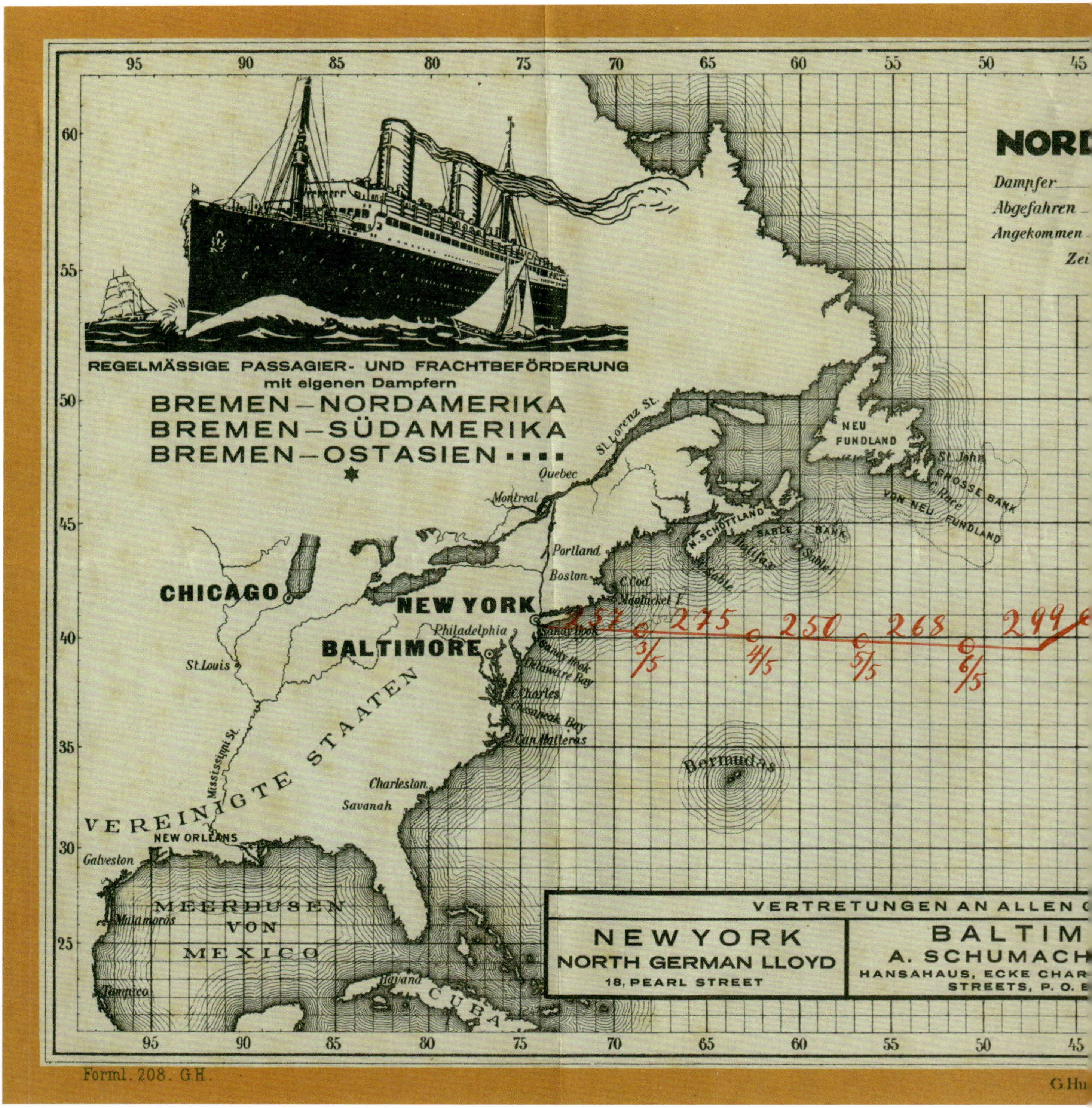
NORD
Dampfer
Abgefahren
Angekommen
Zei
REGELMÄSSIGE PASSAGIER- UND FRACHTBEFÖRDERUNG
mit eigenen Dampfern
BREMEN–NORDAMERIKA
BREMEN–SÜDAMERIKA
BREMEN–OSTASIEN
St. Lorenz St.
Quebec
Montreal
Portland
Boston
C. Cod
Nantucket I.
NEU FUNDLAND
St. John
C. Race
GROSSE BANK VON NEU FUNDLAND
N. SCHOTTLAND
SABLE I. BANK
Halifax
Sable I.
CHICAGO
NEW YORK
Philadelphia
BALTIMORE
Sandy Hook
Delaware Bay
C. Charles
Chesapeak Bay
Cap Hatteras
St. Louis
Mississippi St.
VEREINIGTE STAATEN
Charleston
Savanah
NEW ORLEANS
Galveston
Matamoros
MEERBUSEN VON MEXICO
Tampico
Havana
CUBA
Bermudas
257
275
250
268
299
3/5
4/5
5/5
6/5
VERTRETUNGEN AN ALLEN
NEW YORK
NORTH GERMAN LLOYD
18, PEARL STREET
BALTIM
A. SCHUMACH
HANSAHAUS, ECKE CHAR
STREETS, P. O. B
Forml. 208. G.H.
G.Hu

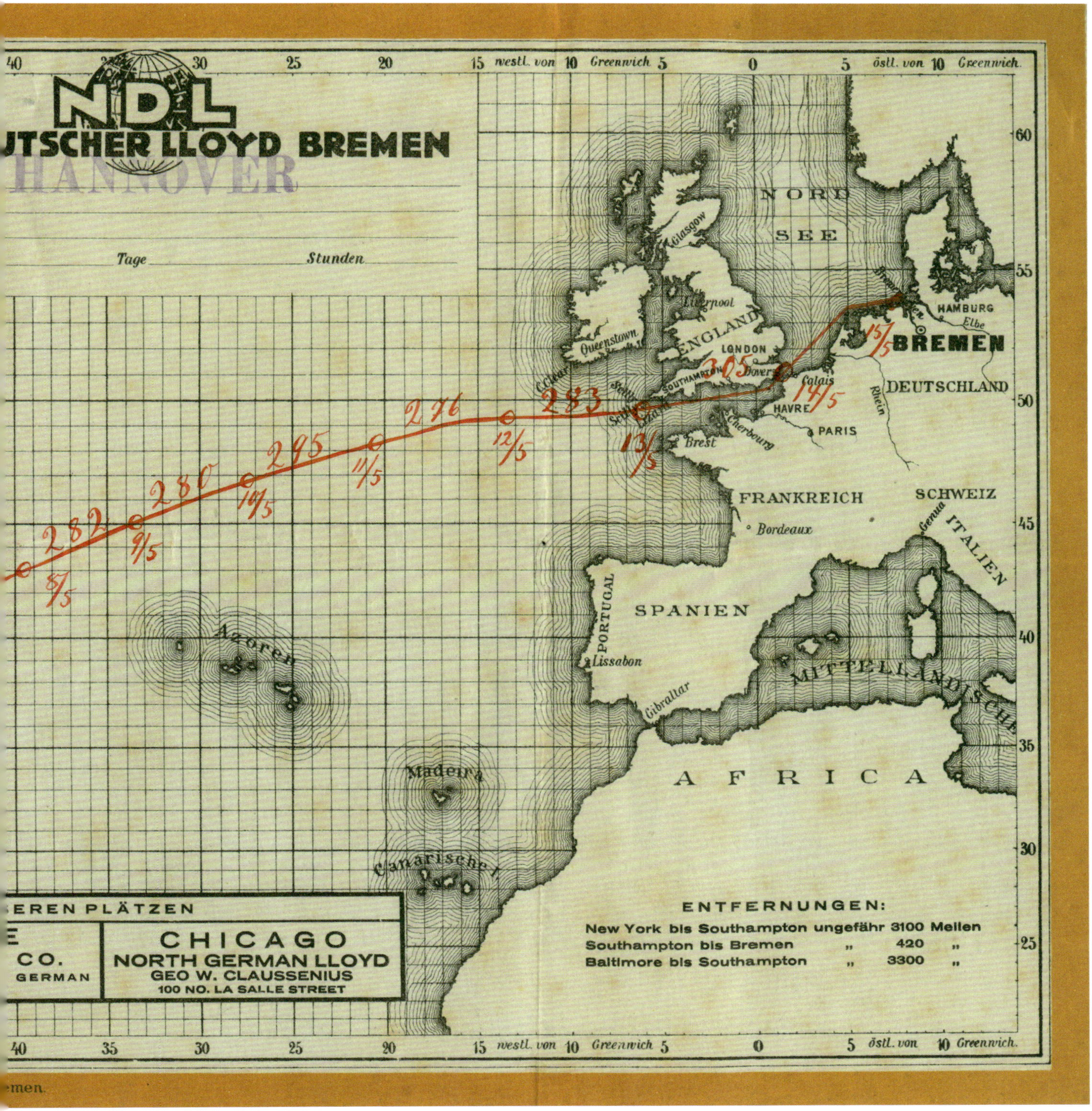

Sammlung Deutsches Auswandererhaus / Collection German Emigration Center

Von einem Passagier eingezeichnete Fahrtstrecke des NDL-Dampfers „Hannover" auf dem Weg von New York nach Bremerhaven mit den täglich zurückgelegten Seemeilen, 03.–15.05.1923. / A passenger has drawn the route of the NGL steamer *Hannover* from New York to Bremerhaven and the number of nautical miles covered each day, 3–15 May 1923.

sellschaft auf. Ihre Schiffsrouten gingen nach Nord- und Südamerika, nach Asien und nach Australien. Millionen Menschen fuhren auf Schiffen des „Norddeutschen Lloyd" in die Neue Welt.

Über Bremerhaven wanderten zwischen 1830 und 1974 insgesamt 7,2 Millionen Menschen aus. Von ihnen stammten 3,4 Millionen aus Osteuropa: Es waren vor allem Polen, Russen, Tschechen, Slowaken, Ungarn und Rumänen, die Deutschland als Transitland nutzten. Die erste große Auswanderungswelle aus Osteuropa setzte Anfang der 1880er Jahre ein und endete mit dem Ersten Weltkrieg. Eine weitere große Welle osteuropäischer Auswanderer schiffte sich Anfang der 1920er Jahre in Bremerhaven ein. Sie vermischten sich auf den Schiffen mit den Deutschen, die aufgrund der Depression nach dem Ersten Weltkrieg und der Wirtschaftskrise zum ersten Mal seit drei Jahrzehnten wieder massenhaft auswanderten. Für viele Europäer wurde der Traum Amerika unerreichbar. Durch die Quotenregelung bei der Einreise, die für die USA seit dem „Quota Act" von 1921 galt, konnte nur eine bestimmte Anzahl Menschen einer Nationalität einreisen. Glück hatte, wer einen Bürgen in den USA hatte: Verwandte oder Freunde, die gegenüber dem Staat schworen, dass sie im Falle von Arbeitslosigkeit oder Geldnot helfen würden, damit der Einwanderer dem amerikanischen Staat nicht zur Last fallen würde. Durch die seit dem frühen 19. Jahrhundert anhaltende Kettenwanderung besaßen sehr viele Deutsche Verwandte, Bekannte oder Freunde in Amerika und so konnten viele trotz der Einreisebeschränkungen einwandern.

Die Gründe für die starke osteuropäische Auswanderung ab 1880 waren vor allem wirtschaftlicher Natur. So wanderten viele beispielsweise aus dem wirtschaftlich von der zaristischen Regierung absichtlich klein gehaltenen Galizien aus, weil sie für sich und ihre Kinder dort keine Zukunft sahen. Auch politische Gründe spielten eine Rolle: Die gescheiterte Revolution von 1905 und die erfolgreiche Novemberrevolution 1918 führten zur Flucht zahlreicher Menschen. Abgefahren sind auch zehntausende von osteuropäischen Juden von Bremerhaven: Sie flohen vor den ab 1881 einsetzenden

and Germans emigrating as a result of the Great Depression shortly after World War I came together on board the ships. In the aftermath of the First World War and the Great Depression, Germans, too, for the first time in three decades, left the country in overwhelming numbers. The dream of America was unattainable for many. The *Quota Act* of 1921 limited annual European immigration to three percent of the number of a nationality group already living in the United States as of 1910. Immigrants who had sponsors vouching for them were lucky indeed—a relative or friend who took an official oath stating that in the event the incoming immigrant was rendered jobless or hard-pressed for money, the sponsor would support that person so as not to burden the U.S. Government. Due to sustained immigration to the United States beginning in the early 1900s many Germans had relatives, friends or acquaintances in America and hence were able to enter the country despite tight immigration restrictions.

The reason for the high number of East European emigrants as of 1880 is to be found in the foundering economy of those countries. Many, for example, left Galicia, a region economically suppressed by the Czarist regime, as they realized there was no future for them or their children in their homeland. Political motives also played a vital role. The revolution of 1905, which had been crushed, and the success of the November Revolution of 1918 forced countless people to flee. Tens of thousands of Jews also fled East Europe by way of Bremerhaven, escaping the pogroms which set in in Russia and in Russian-occupied Poland as of 1881. The pogroms continued up through 1913.

During National Socialism (1933–1945) refugees fleeing the German Reich outnumbered emigrants. Reich President Paul von Hindenburg's appointment of Adolf Hitler, leader of the *National Socialist German Workers' Party* or Nazi Party, as Reich Chancellor of Germany, unleashed the beginning of the Nazi dictatorship, costing the lives of millions all over Europe through late 1945.

Columbuskaje in Bremerhaven: Zurück Bleibende verabschieden ein ablegendes Schiff, um 1920. / The Columbus wharf in Bremerhaven: Those staying behind bid farewell to a ship casting off, about 1920.

Pogromen in Russland und in den von Russland besetzten Teilen Polens. Die Pogrome dauerten bis 1913 an.

In der Zeit des Nationalsozialismus (1933–1945) gab es mehr Flüchtlinge als Auswanderer, die das Deutsche Reich verließen. Am 30. Januar 1933 ernannte der Reichspräsident Paul von Hindenburg Adolf Hitler, den Führer der „Nationalsozialistischen Deutschen Arbeiterpartei" (NSDAP), zum Reichskanzler. Es war der Beginn der nationalsozialistischen Diktatur, die bis zu ihrem Ende 1945 Millionen von Menschen in ganz Europa das Leben kostete.
Am 28. Februar 1933, einen Tag nach dem Brand des Reichstages, beschloss der Reichstag unter Federführung der Nationalsozialisten die „Verordnung zum Schutz von Volk und Staat" („Reichstagsbrandverordnung"), die bis 1945 gültig blieb. In dieser Verordnung wurden die Grundrechte der

February 28, 1933, one day after the Reichstag fire, the deliberate burning down of Germany's parliament building, the new Nazi government used the situation to ban and suppress the German Communist Party by issuing an *Ordinance for the Protection of People and State* which remained in force until 1945 and deprived all citizens of their basic rights. Anybody could now be arrested on suspicion only, imprisoned without trial, without any recourse or right to legal remedy whatsoever. This naturally gave the Nazi Party a free hand to treat people however they pleased, persecuting people on the basis of race or belief. The *Nuremberg Laws,* two racial laws promulgated in

Bürger aufgehoben. Jeder Bürger konnte nun auf bloßen Verdacht hin verhaftet, ohne Urteil in Gefangenschaft gehalten werden und hatte keinerlei Anspruch auf Rechtsmittel. Damit hatten die Nationalsozialisten freie Handhabe gegenüber allen Menschen, die sie aufgrund ihrer „Rasse“ oder Überzeugung verfolgten. Mit den „Nürnberger Gesetzen“ vom 15. September 1935 wurden allen Juden die Vollbürgerrechte entzogen, sie wurden wirtschaftlich ausgegrenzt und ihrer politischen Rechte beraubt. Glaubensjuden und alle, die durch die „Nürnberger Gesetze“ zu Juden erklärt wurden, besaßen nun endgültig keinerlei Rechtssicherheit mehr. Flucht war für viele Menschen die einzige Überlebenschance. Unter der Verfolgung durch die Nationalsozialisten litten vor allem jüdische Bürger sowie nichtjüdische Demokraten, Kommunisten, Schriftsteller und Künstler. Viele gingen zunächst in europäische Nachbarländer, später dann nach Übersee. Die strikten Einwanderungsbestimmungen oder -beschränkungen ließen für viele eine Flucht zur Odyssee durch mehrere Staaten werden.

Nuremberg on September 15, 1935 during a Nazi Party rally, deprived those not of "German or related blood" of German citizenship and made marriage or extra-marital relations illegal between non-Jews and Jews. German Jews were segregated economically and politically. Robbed of all legal security, Germans of Jewish faith and all those proclaimed Jewish on the basis of the *Nuremberg Laws*, realized that the only chance of survival lay in escape. In addition to persecuting Jewish Germans, the Nazis also persecuted non-Jewish democrats, communists, writers and artists. Many escaped to neighboring European countries, only to flee overseas at a later time. The tight immigration regulations and restrictions often turned these journeys into a never-ending odyssey through many states. According to the statistical yearbooks of the Ger-

Antisemitische Parolen und Schmierereien an einem jüdischen Altkleidergeschäft während der Novemberpogrome, München, 09.11.1938. / Anti-Semitic slogans and scribblings on a Jewish thrift shop during the November pogrom, Munich, November 9, 1938.

ullstein bild

Laut den Statistischen Jahrbüchern des Deutschen Reiches emigrierten zwischen 1933 und 1939 insgesamt 117.014 Menschen aus Deutschland. In den Arbeitsberichten des „Zentralausschusses" bzw. der „Reichsvertretung der Deutschen Juden" sind jedoch im gleichen Zeitraum mindestens 234.000 Juden als Flüchtlinge aus Deutschland verzeichnet. Es handelte sich um Glaubensjuden und um Menschen, die nach den „Nürnberger Gesetzen" von 1935 zu Juden ernannt worden waren. In den Statistischen Jahrbüchern des Deutschen Reiches wurden demnach die jüdischen Flüchtlinge unterschlagen.

Vor allem nach der von den Nationalsozialisten benannten „Reichskristallnacht" am 9. November 1938 begann die Weltöffentlichkeit auf die lebensbedrohliche Situation der deutschen Juden aufmerksam zu werden. Die britische Regierung reagierte umgehend: Knapp drei Wochen nach der Pogromnacht begannen die ersten Kindertransporte von Deutschland nach Großbritannien. Mit Kriegsbeginn am 1. September 1939 mussten sie eingestellt werden. Insgesamt konnten etwa 10.000 meist jüdische Kinder gerettet werden. Offiziell wurde im Oktober 1941 ein Auswanderungsverbot im Deutschen Reich erlassen, de facto machte der Ausbruch des Zweiten Weltkrieges die Ausreise für Juden und Nichtjuden unmöglich. Trotzdem gelang zwischen 1939 und 1941 insgesamt 23.000 deutschen Juden die Flucht vor der nationalsozialistischen Vernichtungspolitik.

1945, nach dem Ende des Zweiten Weltkrieges, lebten in ganz Europa nach Schätzungen sieben bis neun Millionen Displaced Persons (DPs): Heimatlose, Entwurzelte, Wanderer wider Willen. Es waren jüdische und nichtjüdische überlebende KZ-Häftlinge, ehemalige Zwangsarbeiter, Fremdarbeiter; auch Kriegsgefangene zählten dazu. Viele von ihnen stammten aus Osteuropa. Zwischen 1945 und 1947 fanden umfassende Repatriierungsmaßnahmen der Alliierten statt und etwa sieben Millionen Heimatlose wurden in ihre ehemaligen Heimatländer zurückgeschickt. Im August 1947 befanden sich noch 1.214.500 Displaced Persons in den

man Reich for the years 1933 to 1939, a total of 117,014 people emigrated from Germany. Interestingly, the reports of the *Central Committee* or the *Reich Representative Committee of German Jews* record that at least 234,000 Jews fled Germany during the same period of time. This figure is restricted to Germans of Jewish faith or those considered Jewish by virtue of the *Nuremberg Laws*. In other words, the statistical yearbooks of the German Reich withheld the number of Jewish fugitives.

Particularly after what the Nazis termed the "Reichskristallnacht" on November 9, 1938, a massive nationwide pogrom in Germany and Austria directed at Jewish citizens and portending the events of the Holocaust, the world gradually became aware of the life-threatening situation of the Jews. The British government was the first to react. Less than three weeks after the nationwide pogrom a program was set up to transport children out of Germany to Great Britain. When the war broke out on September 1, 1939 they had to be stopped. All told, 10,000 mostly Jewish children were saved. In October 1941, an official decree was issued prohibiting citizens to emigrate from the German Reich, but with the outbreak of the war emigration had de facto become impossible for Jews and non-Jews alike. Nevertheless, 23,000 German Jews managed to escape extermination at the hands of Nazi Germany between 1939 and 1941.

By the end of World War II in 1945, an estimated seven to nine million DPs—Displaced Persons who were homeless, uprooted, banished, wanderers against their will—lived throughout Europe. They included Jewish and non-Jewish concentration camp survivors, former forced laborers and foreign workers, many of whom originally came from East Europe. Among them were also prisoners of war. For two years after the war, the Allied forces carried out major repatriation efforts so that by 1947 an estimated seven million DPs had returned to their former native countries. In August 1947, there were still 1,214,500 Displaced

Westzonen Deutschlands und Österreichs, davon allein 747.000 in der US-amerikanischen Zone.
Gerade der Rücktransport in die UdSSR hatte sich als gefährlich erwiesen, denn die sowjetische Regierung betrachtete die Displaced Persons nicht als Opfer, sondern oft auch als Spione des kapitalistischen Westens und schickte sie in die Lager nach Sibirien. Diese Erfahrung und der erschütternde Bericht des vom amerikanischen Präsidenten Truman eingesetzten Beauftragten des „Intergovernmental Committee on Refugees“, Earl G. Harrison, veranlassten die USA und Großbritannien zum Umschwenken in ihrer DP-Politik. Harrison hatte unter anderem dem Präsidenten berichtet: „Wir behandeln die Juden allem Anschein nach nicht anders als die Nazis, nur dass wir sie nicht vernichten.“ [2]
Die jüdischen Displaced Persons nannten sich selbst „She'erith Hapletah“: der überlebende Rest. Oft lebten sie noch jahrelang in den zu DP-Camps umfunktionierten ehemaligen Konzentrationslagern. Unmittelbar nach der Befreiung der Lager hatte es unter den jüdischen Überlebenden einen starken Idealismus und Hoffnung auf die Zukunft gegeben: „Die Toten befahlen zu leben“ (Ze'ev Mankowitz)[3]. Aber die mangelnde internationale Solidarität und die sich über Jahre hinziehende Unentschlossenheit vor allem der US-amerikanischen und britischen Regierungen, wie mit den jüdischen Displaced Persons umzugehen sei, führte zu Resignation. Während sich Großbritannien gegen eine starke jüdische Einwanderung nach Palästina sperrte, wollten die USA bis 1948 eine große Einwanderung in ihr Land nicht zulassen. Letztendlich konnten bis 1952 100.000 jüdische Überlebende mit ihren Kindern nach Nordamerika und 250.000 nach Palästina ausreisen.
Bremerhaven wurde zwischen 1946 und 1952 zum „Port of Embarkation“: Knapp 800.000 jüdische und nichtjüdische Displaced Persons bestiegen hier zwischen 1946 und 1952 die Schiffe, die sie in ein neues Leben bringen sollten.

In den Jahrzehnten nach dem Zweiten Weltkrieg war Deutschland von starken Aus- und Einwanderungswellen

Persons in the western zones of Germany and Austria, of which 747,000 alone were in the American zone.
Transporting Displaced Persons back to Soviet Russia often proved very dangerous as the Soviet regime thought of them not as victims, but as spies from the capitalist West, invariably sending them to labor camps in Siberia. This knowledge and the shocking report by President Truman's agent for the *Intergovernmental Committee on Refugees*, Earl G. Harrison, caused the U.S. and Great Britain to alter their DP policy. Harrison's report to the president noted that, "Evidently we are not treating the Jews any differently than the Nazis did, the only difference being that we don't exterminate them." [2] The displaced Jews referred to themselves as *She'erith Hapletah*—the Holocaust survivors—many of whom lived for years in the former concentration camps. Immediately following the liberation of the concentration camps strong idealism and hope for the future had sprung up among the Jewish survivors. To quote Ze'ev Mankovitz: "The dead commanded that we live." [3] Yet the lack of international solidarity and the protracted indecision on the part of the U.S. and British governments as to how to best deal with Jewish DPs, led to resignation on their part. Whereas Great Britain on the one hand was against widespread Jewish immigration to Palestine, the U.S. on the other hand was against widespread Jewish immigration to the U.S.A., until 1948. Eventually, 100,000 Jewish Holocaust survivors were permitted to enter North America with their children and 250,000 allowed to travel to Palestine.
Bremerhaven evolved into a port of embarkation between 1946 and 1952 with an estimated 800,000 Jewish and non-Jewish DPs boarding ships destined to take them to a new life.

In the decades following the Second World War, Germany was characterized by waves of migratory movement. Between 1945 and 1950 alone, some 7.9 million refugees from regions in Eastern Europe formerly inhabited by ethnic Germans immigrated to the 1949 newly formed Federal Republic of Germany. Their integration in the towns and

ullstein bild

Freudentanz jüdischer Displaced Persons auf dem Bahnhof in München vor ihrer Abreise nach Israel, 13.07.1948. / Jewish Displaced Persons dance for joy at the Munich train station prior to their departure for Israel, July 13, 1948.

geprägt. Allein zwischen 1945 und 1950 kamen knapp 7,9 Millionen Flüchtlinge aus den ehemaligen deutschen Ostgebieten in das Gebiet der 1949 gegründeten Bundesrepublik. Ihre Integration in die Dörfer und Städte zog sich Jahrzehnte hin. Das letzte Vetriebenenlager in der Bundesrepublik wurde erst Anfang der 1970er Jahre aufgelöst.

Neben den auf ihre Ausreise wartenden Displaced Persons gab es viele Deutsche, die das vom Krieg zerstörte Land verlassen wollten. Allerdings gab es bis zur Gründung der Bundesrepublik Deutschland für Deutsche stark reglementierte Einreisemöglichkeiten in die klassischen Einwanderungsländer wie die USA, Kanada und Australien: Auswandern durften nur Ehepartner und Kinder von ausländischen Staatsangehörigen und offiziell anerkannte Verfolgte der nationalsozialistischen Regierung. Tausende der „War Brides“ – Ehefrauen britischer oder US-amerikanischer Soldaten – reisten von Bremerhaven in die Neue Welt.

1949 begannen die westlichen Alliierten die Einreisebeschränkungen für Deutsche zu lockern und zu Beginn der 1950er

cities took years. The last refugee camp in Germany for Displaced Persons wasn't dissolved until the early 1970s.

In addition to the Displaced Persons waiting to leave the country, a large number of Germans also wished to leave war-torn Germany. However, up until the formation of the Federal Republic of Germany immigration restrictions for Germans in the classic countries of immigration, such as the U.S., Canada and Australia were very tight. Only spouses and children of foreign nationals and officially recognized victims of Nazi persecution were allowed to immigrate. Thousands of *war brides*—the wives of British and U.S. soldiers—left from Bremerhaven for the New World.

By 1949 the Western Allied Forces had begun to loosen immigration restrictions for Germans which resulted in a large wave of German emigration during the 1950s. While between

Quellen und Literatur / Sources and References

Aus den mit Hochziffern gekennzeichneten Werken stammen die im Text verwendeten Zitate. / The literature preceded by a number was used for the quotations in this catalogue.

[1] Wittichen, Friedrich Carl / Salzer, Ernst (Hrsg.): Briefe von und an Friedrich Gentz, München, 1909, S. 178.

[2] The Harrison Report; zitiert nach Dinnerstein, Leonard: Britische und amerikanische DP-Politik; in: Fritz Bauer Institut (Hrsg.): Überlebt und unterwegs. Jüdische Displaced Persons im Nachkriegsdeutschland. Jahrbuch zur Geschichte und Wirkung des Holocaust, Frankfurt am Main / New York, 1997, S. 109–117, S. 111.

[3] Mankowitz, Ze'ev, zit. n. Peck, Abraham J.: „Unsere Augen haben die Ewigkeit gesehen". Erinnerung und Identität der She'erith Hapletah; in: Fritz Bauer Institut (Hrsg.), wie Anmerkung 2, S. 27–49, S. 35.

Zahlen und Prozentangaben entstammen folgenden Werken: / Figures and percentages are from the following sources:

Arbeitsberichte des Zentralausschusses der deutschen Juden für Hilfe und Aufbau bei der Reichsvertretung der Deutschen Juden für die Jahre 1933–1941.

Chicago Historical Society (bearb. von): "Population Figures by Single Years of the City of Chicago," 1988.

Craig, Gordon A.: *Germany 1866–1945*, Oxford, 1980.

Hoerder, Dirk / Knauf, Diethelm (Hrsg.): Aufbruch in die Fremde. Europäische Auswanderung nach Übersee, Bremen, 1992.

Howard, Robert P.: *Illinois. A History of the Prairie State*, Grand Rapids, 1972.

Nerger-Focke, Karin: Die deutsche Amerikaauswanderung nach 1945, Stuttgart, 1995.

Ritter, Gerhard A. / Tenfelde, Klaus: Arbeiter im Deutschen Kaiserreich 1871 bis 1914, Bonn, 1992.

Statistisches Bundesamt Deutschland: Wanderungsstatistik. Wanderungen über die Grenzen Deutschlands 1950–2004, Wiesbaden, 2005.

Statistisches Reichsamt (Hrsg.): Statistik des Deutschen Reiches, Berlin, Jahrgänge 1933–1941.

Wehler, Hans-Ulrich: Deutsche Gesellschaftsgeschichte, Bd. 1: Vom Feudalismus des Alten Reiches bis zur Defensiven Modernisierung der Reformära 1700–1815, München, 1996.

Wehler, Hans-Ulrich: Deutsche Gesellschaftsgeschichte, Bd. 2: Von der Reformära bis zur industriellen und politischen „Deutschen Doppelrevolution" 1815–1845/49, München, 1995.

DEN DETAILS AUF DER SPUR / INSIGHT INTO THE DETAILS

35

DEN DETAILS AUF DER SPUR
Objekt- und Bilderwelten im Deutschen Auswandererhaus

INSIGHT INTO THE DETAILS
Exhibits and Pictures at the German Emigration Center

Bilder, Objekte, Faksimiles oder Nachbauten: Im Deutschen Auswandererhaus dienen alle Bestandteile von Inszenierung und Vermittlung den wichtigsten Ausstellungsinhalten – den Biographien. Die Besucher erleben die Geschichte der Auswanderung hautnah. Sie betreten Bilderwelten, in denen die wichtigsten Stationen einer Auswanderung Plattform sind für die Darstellung der Biographien. Bewusst hat das Deutsche Auswandererhaus dort, wo keine Originale zur Verfügung standen, die Szenerie mit präzisen, liebevollen Nachbauten komplettiert. Originale und Faksimiles atmen gemeinsam den Zeitgeist und wecken mit der im Hintergrund bleibenden Museumstechnik die Lust an der Entdeckung. Geschichte wird lebendig. Und die Sammlung wächst. Durch Ankäufe, Ersteigerungen und vor allen Dingen durch Schenkungen vieler Privatpersonen wird das Fundament dieses jungen Themenmuseums gestärkt.

Pictures, objects, facsimiles or reproductions—all of these impart and present the focal point of the German Emigration Center, the biographies. Visitors relive the history of emigration up close, entering a world of images in which the main stations of emigration act as a stage for illustrating the biographies. Where no originals were to be had, the German Emigration Center deliberately used precise and carefully worked reproductions. The originals and facsimiles act in concert, breathing the spirit of emigration, while the museum technology, concealed in the background, makes the exhibition—and history—come alive, arousing interest and curiosity. Thanks to acquisitions by means of purchase and auctions, and most particularly by private donations the museum collection continues to grow, reinforcing the foundation of this young theme museum and putting it on a firm footing.

Stiftung Deutsches Auswandererhaus / German Emigration Center Foundation

Bestimmte Gemälde sind Inkunabeln für jedes Museum: Sie zeigen den Anfang von etwas, das Geschichte machen wird. Felix Schlesingers Ölgemälde „In der Pass- und Polizeistube vor der Auswanderung" entstand 1859. Es rückt ein existentielles Dokument in den Mittelpunkt: den Pass. Ohne Pass konnte man damals nicht legal auswandern – und kann es heute nicht. Hoffnung und Sehnsucht hängen an einem Stück Papier. / Every museum has certain paintings which are incunabula, showing the beginning of something that will one day make history. Felix Schlesinger´s oil painting *The Passport and Police Dispatch Prior to Emigration* dates back to 1859 and focuses on a vital document—the passport. Just as now, no one could legally emigrate without this invaluable document. All hope and longing attached to a tiny piece of paper.

Gestiftet vom / Donation:
Initiativkreis Deutsches Auswandererhaus e.V.

H. Dehn

H. Dehn

Stille Zeugen / Silent Witnesses

Still und würdevoll stehen menschengroße Puppen im historischen Teil der Dauerausstellung und erinnern an Auswanderer vergangener Epochen. 45 dieser Puppen stehen an der Kaje: Jede hat eine individuelle Körperhaltung. Die eine zeigt Angst, die andere freudige Angespanntheit ob des anlegenden Schiffes. Wieder eine andere zeigt einen Vater, der um seinen kleinen Sohn bangt, er möge nicht ins Wasser fallen. Alle sind fasziniert von der mächtigen Bordwand, die sich vor ihnen erhebt: Besucher und Puppen schauen in dieselbe Richtung.

Die Puppen stehen – so wie Menschen – teils in Gruppen aneinander gedrängt, teils allein. Für die Besucher nicht auf den ersten Blick erkennbar, hat ihre Verteilung einen Sinn: Sie repräsentiert die drei großen Zeitabschnitte der Auswanderung und bietet einen Einblick in die Geschichte der Bekleidung der „einfachen" Leute aus 150 Jahren. Alle Stoffe und Materialien entsprechen den damals verwendeten; selbst die Unterwäsche der Puppen wurde individuell angefertigt.

The permanent exhibition features life-size dolls dressed in historic garb, standing in quiet dignity. They remind us of the men, women and children of bygone days who embarked on a trip into the unknown—emigration.

Forty-five silent witnesses, gathered on the wharf, each with individual poses and facial expressions—some anxious and fearful of boarding the moored ship, others excited about what lies ahead. One man watches his little son, afraid he might fall in the water. All forty-five are fascinated by the tall side of the mighty ship—the eyes of museum visitors and silent witnesses alike are drawn to this powerful image. While not immediately evident to the visitor, the dolls are grouped into three categories, representing the three main periods of emigration, and hence the history of ordinary people's clothing over the course of 150 years. All the materials used for making their costumes, even the underpinnings, conform to the period the doll represents.

DAH

DAH

Verborgene Museumstechnik
Concealed Museum Technology

„Bitte drehen Sie den Wasserhahn zu." Subtil und unaufdringlich wird dazu aufgefordert, neugierig zu sein, spielerisch auszuprobieren und so Wissen zu vertiefen. Ein Wasserbecken mit integriertem Bildschirm, ein deutlich hörbares Tropfen im Raum sind Teil der Inszenierung, die einen Waschraum für Auswanderer auf dem Schnelldampfer „Lahn" darstellt. Dreht der Besucher am Wasserhahn, verschwindet der Bildschirmschoner und Informationen über die Hygiene an Bord werden verfügbar. Der Verzicht auf Maus oder Scrollrad als Bedienelemente sind Teil des Konzepts.

In anderen Bereichen steht die Individualisierung des Museumsrundgangs im Mittelpunkt. Bereits am Eingang erhält der Besucher eine Plastikkarte, die mit RFID-Technik (Radio Frequency Identification) ausgestattet ist. Auf ihr ist eine Auswandererbiographie hinterlegt. Mit Hilfe dieser Karte kann der Besucher auf der „Reise" durch die Ausstellung an Hör- und Rechnerstationen etwas über den Verlauf der Auswanderung der jeweiligen Biographie erfahren. Hinter den Kulissen stecken innovative Technik, schnelle Netzwerke und aufwändige Programmierung – der Besucher sieht davon fast nichts. Die historische Inszenierung wird nicht gestört und der Besucher kann ganz in die Stimmung der Auswanderung eintauchen.

Nur im „Forum Migration" wird die Technik nicht versteckt. Der Bruch ist Konzept, denn nun ist der Besucher in der heutigen Zeit angekommen und wird mit aktuellen Fakten zum Thema empfangen.

"Please turn off the faucet." A subtle, unassuming request for the visitor to display curiosity by playing with the faucet and simultaneously increasing his or her knowledge. A sink with an integrated screen, a clearly audible drip in the room, all part of the setting in the washrooms for emigrants on board the fast steamship *Lahn*. Once the visitor turns the handle, the screen saver disappears revealing information about sanitary facilities and conditions on board the ship. No computer mouse or scroll wheel is needed to operate these elements.

Other areas focus on individualizing the museum tour. For example, at the entrance visitors receive a plastic card equipped with RFID technology (radio frequency identification) which contains the biography of an emigrant. During their tour of the museum visitors may use this card at certain audio and media stations to hear or learn more about "their" emigrant's trip to the New World. Behind the scenes, invisible to the visitor, are the innovative technology, fast networks and complex programming operating these special stations. Thus, the historic presentation is not disrupted and visitors can immerse themselves in the prevalent mood. *Forum Migration* is the only area where technology is clearly visible and this quite intentionally. On entering this room the visitor re-enters the present and is confronted with current facts and figures on migration.

DAH

Verlust des Gleichgewichts: die Überfahrt
Losing One's Balance: The Ocean Crossing

Über die Gangway ist der Besucher hinauf in den Bauch des Schiffes gelangt. Im Schiffsgang stellen Bullaugen die einzige Verbindung zur Außenwelt dar. Manche von ihnen sind geöffnet, auf eingebauten Bildschirmen laufen Filmsequenzen vom Meer. Durch die Wahl der passenden Perspektive und das Auf und Ab der Wellen entsteht der Eindruck, auf voller Fahrt zu sein. Außerdem spielt die Bewegung dem menschlichen Gleichgewichtsorgan einen Streich. Der Boden scheint nachzugeben und die gewohnte stabile Grundlage verloren zu gehen. Nicht zur Interaktion dient hier die Technik, sondern zur Perfektionierung der Illusion.

The gangway leads the visitor up into the belly of the ship. Once inside, bull-eyes constitute the only connection to the outside world. Some are open and project film sequences at sea on built-in screens. The choice of perspective and the wave movement create the impression of being on board a ship at high sea, thereby playing a trick on the organ of equilibrium in the inner ear. The floor seems to sway under one's feet, the feeling of stability is lost. Whereas in the above examples technology enhanced interaction, we witness here how technology contributes to perfecting an illusion.

Keine Reise ohne Koffer
Have Suitcase Will Travel

Überseekisten, große Körbe, Koffer, Taschen sind das Attribut des Auswanderers wie Reisenden. Sie stehen an der Kaje, sind im Gepäckraum des Schiffs verladen, vor der Ankunft an Deck hoch aufgestapelt. Es sind Originale und detailgetreue Nachbildungen historischer Gepäckstücke aus dem 19. und 20. Jahrhundert. Sie dokumentieren die Kultur des Reisens, sie erzählen aber auch von den Auswanderern und ihrer Herkunft: Form und Material zeigen, ob der Besitzer als Handwerker, Tagelöhner oder Bauer ausgewandert ist oder ob er aus wohlhabenderen Verhältnissen stammte. Kratzer und Schrammen, Plaketten und bunte Gepäckanhänger verweisen auf lange Reisen voller Umwege und Zwischenstationen.
Angesichts der Kisten und Koffer kann man nur erahnen, wie viele Lebensgeschichten der sorgsam verpackte Inhalt preisgeben könnte.

Steamer trunks, oversize baskets, suitcases, bags—all of these objects were among the baggage carried by emigrants. Baggage is stacked on the wharf, loaded on the ship, stacked on deck shortly prior to arrival. Some of the pieces on exhibit are original, others are one-to-one reproductions of historic baggage from the nineteenth and twentieth centuries documenting the culture of overseas travel, revealing tales about emigrants and where they came from. The shape and material disclose whether the owner was a craftsman, day laborer or peasant or whether he or she came from a wealthy background. Scratches and marks, emblems and colorful baggage tags indicate long trips with stops in several places. Given the number of boxes and suitcases one can only begin to imagine the diversity and number of life stories the carefully stowed contents of each would disclose.

H. Dehn

DAH

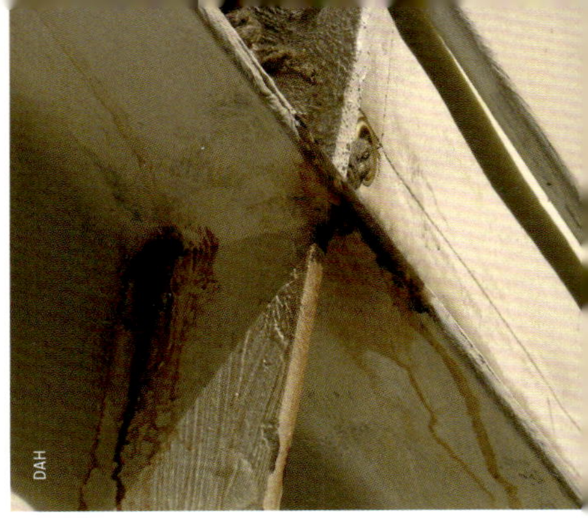

Rost oder die Kunst der Theatermalerei
Rust or the Art of Painting Stage Sets

Was sehen Besucher in Museen? „Alte" Dinge, oft allerdings bis zum „Neuzustand" restauriert; Fotos, die eine gesehene, augenblickliche Situation abbilden. Oder mediale Erläuterungen, die die Sprache der Museumskuratoren unterstützen. Im Deutschen Auswandererhaus wird die Aussage durch inszenierte Einbauten unterstützt, die das Original illustrativ in seinen Bestimmungsort transponieren.
Die Fertigkeiten der alten Kunst der Theatermalerei sind eingesetzt, um den Besucher in die historische Situation zu versetzen. Rost, Schmutzflecken, Wasserspuren, Tropfnasen und Gebrauchsspuren helfen, die Geschichte der Auswanderer zu erzählen.

What do visitors see when they go to a museum? "Old" things, frequently restored to take on the appearance of being new; photos which depict an image of a split-second situation as seen through one individual's eyes. Or media explanations elaborating on what museum curators have said. Their statements are underscored by presentations integrated into the exhibition illustrating bygone eras and transporting the viewer back in history and time.
The professional skill of painting stage sets was employed at the German Emigration Center for the purpose of transporting the viewer back in history and time. Rust, smudges, water stains, runny noses, and marks of use all contribute to tell the story of the emigrants.

Der Patentklappwaschtisch
The Patented Fold-Up Washstand

Ein Patentklappwaschtisch aus den 1920er Jahren steht mitten in der nachgebildeten III. Klasse-Kabine des Liners „Columbus". Warum ein Original, wenn doch die Kulisse so täuschend echt aussieht? Vereinzelt eingefügte Originale laden die Inszenierung auf. Als Symbole stehen sie für eine Epoche, eine besondere Entwicklung oder ein Ereignis. Der Patentklappwaschtisch beispielsweise ist ein Symbol unerwarteten Luxus'. Die meisten Auswanderer entstammten einfachen Verhältnissen. Ein Waschbecken in der Kabine anstelle eines außerhalb gelegenen Waschhauses galt daher als etwas Besonderes, auch wenn es noch kein fließendes Wasser gab.

A patented fold-up washstand dating back to the 1920s stands smack in the middle of the reproduced steerage liner cabin *Columbus*. Why an original object when a backdrop can look so deceptively authentic? The sporadic positioning of original pieces loosens up the setting and acts as a symbol of a certain era, development or event. The patent fold-up washstand for example is a symbol of unexpected luxury. The majority of emigrants invariably came from very poor backgrounds. To find a washstand in their cabins instead of an external washhouse was very special indeed, even if there still was no running water.

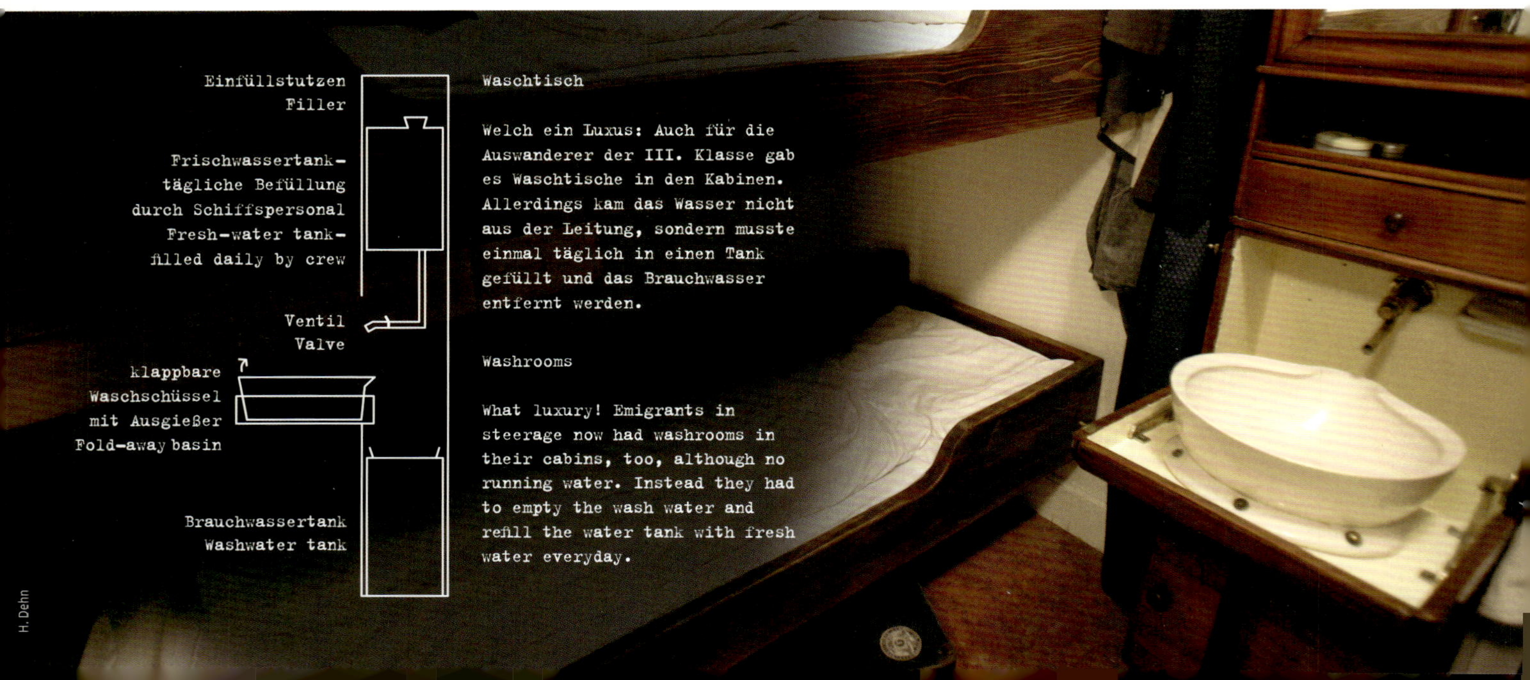

Lebenswege / Paths of Life

Namen von Auswanderern und ihre Geschichten in der „Galerie der 7 Millionen": Eine Wand mit unzähligen Schubladen und kleinen Vitrinen lässt den Umfang einer solchen Sammlung erahnen. Viele Fächer sind sorgfältig mit Namen und Jahreszahlen beschriftet. Neugierig sucht man nach bestimmten Personen und öffnet Schubladen. Wie Schatzkästchen bewahren sie persönliche Andenken, Dokumente und Fotos, die die Lebensumstände der Auswanderer bis zum Aufbruch erzählen. Andere enthalten nur den Auszug aus einer Passagierliste, wieder andere sind noch leer. Dieses Archiv ist besonders, es lebt und wächst; es lädt nicht nur zum Finden und Forschen ein, es veranlasst viele Besucher, an ihre eigene Auswanderung oder die ihrer Vorfahren zu denken und diese Geschichten für unsere Sammlung zur Verfügung zu stellen.

Names of emigrants and their stories fill the *Gallery of the 7 Million*. A wall with countless drawers and small display cases gives a fair indication of the extent of the collection. A large number of drawers are carefully inscribed with names and dates. The visitor's curiosity is aroused, names are sought, drawers are opened, revealing tiny treasure chests full of personal mementos, documents and photos which contribute to drawing a picture of an emigrant and the conditions he or she lived in. Some drawers contain nothing more than an excerpt from the passenger manifest. Still others are empty, waiting to be filled. This archive is very special in that it lives and grows, inviting visitors to search and find, and other visitors to relive their own emigration or to take a moment to think of their ancestors' emigration, and, ultimately, to their possibly donating stories, documents or other items to our collection.

DAH

Schiffe im Schiff / Ships Inside the Ship

Drei Schiffsmodelle in einer Transportkiste stehen im Gepäckraum des Dampfschiffes „Lahn": das Segelschiff „Bremen" von 1854, das Dampfschiff „Lahn" von 1887 und der Liner „Columbus" von 1923. Nicht nur der Größenvergleich soll die Besucher staunen lassen. Entgegen der jahrhundertealten Tradition, Schiffsmodelle als Prunkstücke an exponierter Stelle zu präsentieren, werden sie hier bewusst unspektakulär, en passant gezeigt: Als Teil einer Schiffsladung stehen die verkleinerten Spiegelbilder in einer Transportkiste und wie die Originale tragen auch sie dieselben Spuren, die jahrzehntelanger Sturm und schwere See hinterlassen haben.

Three ship models are displayed inside a shipping crate in the luggage compartment of the steamship *Lahn*—the sailing ship *Bremen* from 1854, the steamship *Lahn* from 1887 and the liner *Columbus* from 1923. The varying sizes of these three ships will certainly cause surprise and astonishment. Contrary to the age-old tradition of showcasing ship models we purposely decided to present them in an entirely unspectacular way, in passing, so to speak. The scaled-down reflections of all three models inside a shipping crate are part of a shipload, and just as the originals they too bear the marks that decades of heavy seas and storms have left on them.

DAH

Welcome Home

Verdichtet in eindrucksvollen Bildern stellt der Film von Ciro Cappellari sechs Vertreter verschiedener Einwanderergenerationen vor und lässt so die Geschichte der Auswanderung bis in die Gegenwart lebendig werden. Er reflektiert die unterschiedlichen Erwartungen und Träume, Erfahrungen und Erlebnisse dieser Menschen in ihrer neuen Heimat und lässt den Zuschauer emotional daran teilhaben. Wie ein Erzählfaden binden historische Filmaufnahmen vom Leben an Bord während der Überfahrt die Begegnungen im heutigen Amerika zusammen. Die individuellen Geschichten zeigen auch, dass das Thema Migration immer aktuell sein wird.

In his film *Welcome Home* Ciro Cappellari captures impressive images of six men and women who represent generations of immigrants to the United States, creating a compact story of immigration down through the ages. The viewer is emotionally involved in the expectations and dreams they had, what they learned and experienced in their new home. Historical film shots from life on board a ship during a transatlantic crossing are woven into encounters and experiences in present-day America. The individual stories also show that migration was and is a current topic.

Historische Meilensteine
Milestones in History

Eine Frage steht am Anfang: Warum sind sie gegangen? Antworten sammeln und bewahren, Geschichte entdecken zwischen vergilbten Aktendeckeln, staubigen Archivkartons und provisorischen Bilderwänden. Geschichte wird immer wieder neu geschrieben und interpretiert. Geschichtsquellen sind Dokumente, Bilder und Objekte. In den fünf historischen Meilensteinen sind Zeitdokumente, Schlüsselbilder und Objekte in Vitrinen gesammelt, die gesellschaftliche und politische Gründe für Auswanderung zeigen. Der Besucher kann und soll sie selbst interpretieren und mit dem Heute vergleichen. Wer das nicht möchte, kann sich eine Interpretation in der im Meilenstein integrierten Hörstation erzählen lassen.
Mit der Darstellung der großen Gesellschaftsgeschichte stehen die historischen Meilensteine in der „Galerie der 7 Millionen" den tausenden gesammelten Lebenserinnerungen von Auswanderern gegenüber. Die große Geschichte und die kleinen, persönlichen Geschichten bilden zusammen ein Ganzes.

The beginning is marked by the question: Why did they leave? Collecting and storing answers, discovering stories inside folders, yellowed by age, dusty storage boxes and makeshift photo galleries. History is written, re-written, and interpreted. Documents, pictures, and objects are all sources of history. The objects displayed in the glass cabinets, one for each milestone in history, reflect the social and political environment which led to emigration. The visitor may and should interpret them and compare them to today's environment, or listen to the interpretation on the audio station integrated into each of the five milestones.
The five milestones in the *Gallery of the 7 Million* illustrate specific periods in history connected to the stories of the thousands of living memories collected and stored in this room. The big story and all the little personal stories come together to form a whole.

BILDER DER AUSSTELLUNG / PICTURES OF THE EXHIBITION

43

Wartehalle / Waiting Hall

In der ab 1869 gebauten Wartehalle warteten die Auswanderer auf die Abfahrt ihres Schiffes. Die Wartehalle der Reederei „Norddeutscher Lloyd“ steht nicht mehr, könnte heute von außen aber vielleicht so aussehen. / Emigrants awaited departure of their ship in the Waiting Hall, built after 1869. Although the Waiting Hall built by *North German Lloyd* Shipping Line no longer exists, it is highly probable that it resembled this.

DAH

An der Kaje / On the Wharf

Bremerhaven, 1888: Regen fällt. Auswanderer aus allen Regionen Europas drängen sich an der Kaje. Ihre Stimmen vermischen sich mit den Geräuschen des Hafens. Vor ihnen erhebt sich die Bordwand der „Lahn". Der Schnelldampfer ist zum Ablegen bereit. / Bremerhaven, 1888: It's raining. Emigrants from all over Europe crowd the wharf. Their voices mingle with sounds from the port. The side of the *Lahn* rises high above them. The fast steamship is ready to cast off.

S. Volk

Galerie der 7 Millionen / Gallery of the 7 Million

Woher kamen sie? Wohin gingen sie? 2.000 Namen sind hier versammelt. Briefe, Fotos, Passagierlisten und Erinnerungsstücke geben Auskunft, warum die Auswanderer Europa verließen. Historische Bilder, Dokumente und Hörtexte erklären die politischen, wirtschaftlichen und gesellschaftlichen Ursachen der Auswanderung zwischen 1830 und 1974. / Where did they come from? Where were they going? Two thousand names are stored here. Letters, photos and personal mementos reveal why these men and women left Europe. Historic pictures, documents, passenger lists and audio texts explain the political, economic and social environment which provoked mass emigration between 1830 and 1974.

W. Hühmacher

Überfahrt / The Crossing

Schiffsräume auf einem Segelschiff, einem Schnelldampfer und einem Liner lassen die Besucher nacherleben, wie es den Auswanderern während der Atlantiküberfahrt ergangen ist. / Accommodations on board a sailing ship, a fast steamship and an ocean liner bring home the hardships of the transatlantic crossing.

DAH

H. Dehn

H. Dehn

Ellis Island

Erleichterung, Hoffnung und Ungewissheit begleiten die ersten Schritte der Amerikaauswanderer: Meist hieß ihr Ziel New York. Mehr als 16 Millionen Menschen passierten die Einwanderungsstation Ellis Island vor Manhattan zwischen 1892 und 1954. Nach medizinischer Untersuchung und einer Befragung durch Inspektoren entschied sich hier, wer einreisen durfte und wer zurückgeschickt wurde. / Relief, hope and uncertainty were the steady companions of immigrants first arriving in America, the majority of whom chose New York as their destination. From 1892 to 1954 more than 16 million people passed through the Ellis Island receiving station just beyond Manhattan. Whether they were allowed to enter the U.S.A. or deported back to their native countries depended on a medical examination and questioning by an immigration inspector.

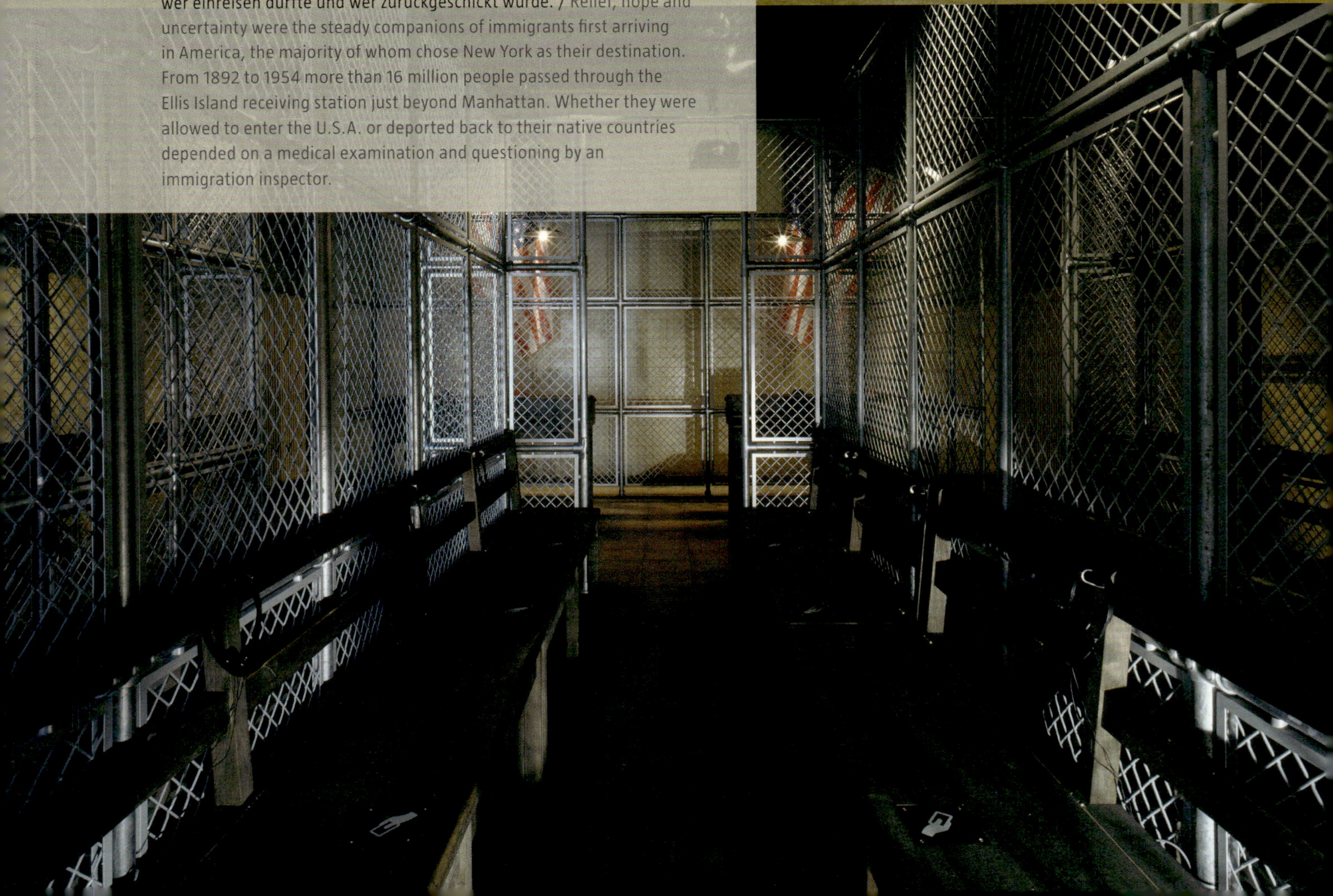

W. Huthmacher

W. Huthmacher

Ocean Cinema

Das Ocean Cinema erinnert an die prächtigen Kinosäle der 1920er Jahre. Hier werden die bewegenden Filme „Welcome Home" und „24h Buenos Aires" des Dokumentarfilmers Ciro Cappellari gezeigt.
The Ocean Cinema is reminiscent of the magnificent movie theaters of the 1920s. And this is where *Welcome Home* and *24h Buenos Aires*, the moving films by film-maker Ciro Cappellari, are shown.

W. Huthmacher

Forum Migration

Migration ist ein Thema der Gegenwart. Hier werden aktuelle globale Wanderungsbewegungen und Aspekte des Zusammenlebens verschiedener Kulturen beleuchtet. In fünf verschiedenen Datenbanken können Besucher nach ausgewanderten Vorfahren recherchieren.

Migration is a current topic. Forum Migration focuses on current global migratory movements and aspects of different cultures living together in one society. Visitors have access to five different databases to research ancestors.

W. Huthmacher

DAH

Kindermuseum

Spielend lernen: Kinder von sechs bis zwölf Jahren haben hier ihren eigenen Erlebnisbereich und können sich in das Abenteuer Auswanderung stürzen: Gold waschen, malen und basteln. / Learning by playing: a special theme area for children aged six to twelve where they can jump into the adventure of emigration, washing gold, painting and making things.

DAH

BIOGRAPHIEN / BIOGRAPHIES

59

AUSWANDERN IN DIE USA UND NACH BRASILIEN

EMIGRATION TO THE U.S.A. AND BRAZIL

BRIGITTE LANDES

Können wir uns wirklich noch vorstellen, was es vor inzwischen fast zwei Jahrhunderten bedeutete auszuwandern? Kein Film, kein Fernsehen, keine Fotografien, keine Werbeprospekte, keine Bilder gab es von der fremden Neuen Welt. Die Vorstellungen beruhten einzig und allein auf Schilderungen in Briefen von Freunden oder Verwandten, die den großen Schritt über den Ozean bereits gewagt hatten. Amerika, das bedeutete Freiheit, Unabhängigkeit, viel Land, wenig Leute, die Möglichkeit, eine Existenz aufzubauen, die in Europa, in Deutschland nicht mehr zu leben war. Größer als alle Phantasie, sich einen neuen Anfang, ein anderes neues Leben zu imaginieren, muss die Not gewesen sein, die viele zum Aufbruch zwang. Über fast allen Lebensläufen könnte das Motto aus dem Märchen „Die Bremer Stadtmusikanten" stehen: „Etwas Besseres als den Tod findest du überall."

Wie viel Phantasie brauchen wir heute, uns vorzustellen, dass

Are we honestly capable of imagining what it meant to emigrate almost two centuries ago? Movies and television, photographs and advertising brochures—none of these modern-day media existed at that time. Consequently, people had no means of visualizing the remoteness and strangeness of the New World. Descriptions in letters written by friends and relatives who bravely ventured across the Atlantic to set up a new life for themselves were the sole source of information. America was a synonym for freedom, independence, endless land, sparse population and the opportunity to establish the kind of livelihood that was no longer possible in Germany or Europe. The destitution and desperation these people suffered was evidently immense and the driving force behind the hundreds of thousands of men and women who left their native countries, seeking a life of opportunity in the New World. The famed motto from Grimms' fairy tale *The Bremen Town Musicians*, "You can find something better than death

Hin nach Texas! / Wo der Stern im blauen Felde / Eine neue Welt verkündet, / Jedes Herz für Recht und Freiheit / Und für Wahrheit froh entzündet, / Dahin sehnt mein Herz sich ganz. / Goldner Stern du bist der Bote / Unsres neuen schön'ren Lebens; / Denn was freie Herzen hoffen, / Hofften sie noch nie vergebens. / Off to Texas! / Sole star shining in a field of blue / Heralding in a world all new, / Hearts beat for freedom, justice and truth, / 'Tis there I long to be. / Golden star, messenger of / A life so new and wonderful; / For that which free hearts hope / shall never be in vain.

Aus: / Freely adapted from: Hoffmann von Fallersleben: „Der Stern von Texas", 1847.

eine ganze Familie oder auch nur ein einzelner junger Mensch sein kleines Dorf, die Menschen, die ihm vertraut sind, verlässt, ein Pferd oder eine Kutsche besteigt oder sich zu Fuß auf den Weg zu einem Hafen, zum Meer macht, wo große Segelschiffe in sechs bis zwölf Wochen über den großen Ozean in das unbekannte Amerika fuhren, kaum Hab und Gut, nur Erinnerung im Gepäck und viel, viel Hoffnung und Mut. Herumziehende Werber propagierten die Auswanderung und fanden Gehör bei den von Hungersnöten geplagten Bauern, bei den durch die Industrielle Revolution um ihre Arbeit gebrachten Handwerkern, bei Anhängern der Französischen Revolution, demokratisch gesinnten Menschen, auch bei Abenteurern oder in Gemeinden, die ihre Zuchthäusler abschieben wollten. Schon immer wussten Menschen, wie man aus Notlagen, Kriegen und Naturkatastrophen Geschäfte machen kann.

Ab Mitte des 19. Jahrhunderts, seit es die Eisenbahn und das Dampfschiff gab, wurde der in jedem einzelnen Fall gewiss schwere Entschluss, die Heimat für immer zu verlassen, etwas erleichtert. Die erste große Auswanderungswelle begann.

Heimlich schlummerte wohl in jedem der Traum vom großen Glück, jedenfalls von einem Leben mit weniger Armut und Mühsal. Aber Schlaraffenland sei es nicht, schreibt **Johann Dietel**, der jüngste Sohn einer Bauernfamilie aus Kleinlosnitz in Oberfranken, der 1848 mit 18 Jahren mit seiner Schwester Margaretha nach Oswego in Iowa ausgewandert war, in seinen Briefen nach Hause: „Wenn man zu etwas kommen

...kaum Hab und Gut, nur Erinnerung im Gepäck und viel, viel Hoffnung und Mut. / ...with not a penny to your name and no possessions to speak of, nothing but memories and hope and courage to stand one in good stead.

everywhere," seemed to apply to everyone who emigrated. It would require a great amount of imagination today for us to conjure up the reality of an entire family or a single individual on the verge of adulthood leaving the village that is home, taking leave of friends and relatives who are dear, traveling by carriage or on horseback, or even setting out on a long journey by foot to a seaport in order to board a great sailing ship, enduring a perilous ocean crossing lasting from six to 12 weeks, and finally setting foot in a strange country named America, with not a penny to your name and no possessions to speak of, nothing but memories and hope and courage to stand one in good stead.

Traveling solicitors propagating emigration at the time naturally gained the attention of peasant farmers struck by famine, craftsmen rendered jobless by the onset of the Industrial Revolution, partisans of the French Revolution, citizens leaning towards democracy, and of course, adventurers as well as communities anxious to deport jail convicts. Mankind has never ceased to cash in on human plight and misery, wars and natural disasters.

With the advent of the railroad and the steamship in the mid-1900s, the weighty decision of abandoning one's hometown forever became somewhat easier. And so began the first major wave of emigration.

Everybody dreamed secretly of making a great fortune, or at least they

Oberfränkisches Bauernhofmuseum Kleinlosnitz

Johann Dietel

*** 07.01.1830 Kleinlosnitz, Oberfranken (heute / today: Bayern / Bavaria);**
† 21.07.1892 Oswego, Iowa, USA

Johann Dietel mit seiner Frau Elisabeth (1832–1902) und den Töchtern Margret (1854–1943) und Helen (1856–1948). / Johann Dietel and his wife Elisabeth (1832–1902), with their daughters Margret (1854–1943) and Helen (1856–1948).

will, muss man auch in Amerika arbeiten." Und: „Ein Lump ist auch hier nichts wert!" Johann Dietel gehörte 1848 zu einer Gruppe von 30 Menschen, die sich aus dem Münchberger Raum im Fichtelgebirge auf den Weg nach Amerika machten. Das muss man sich einmal ganz genau vorstellen: Aus einer kleinen ländlichen Region wandern an einem Tag gleichzeitig 30 Menschen aus, für immer! Das ist kein Ausflug oder eine Pauschalreise! Bis Einbeck zog der Trupp zu Fuß und per Kutsche: „Eisenbahn benutzen!" rät Johann seinem älteren Bruder. Dieser folgt den Geschwistern ein Jahr später. In Oswego angekommen, stellt er die Distanz, die zwischen ihnen liegt von Kleinlosnitz bis nach Oswego in Stunden dar: „Von Kleinlosnitz nach Bremerhaven sind es 173, von da an über das atlantische Meer bis New York 2200, von da bis Oswego 680 Stunden, im ganzen 3053 deutsche Stunden." Trotz Eisenbahn eine Reise von immer noch gut drei Monaten! Johann Konrad Dietel, der ältere Bruder, brauchte, wie andere Quellen belegen, für seine Reise nach Oswego zwei Monate. Ein Jahr später fuhr er, der in Amerika nicht Fuß fassen konnte, den ganzen Weg zurück nach Hause.

dreamed of a life marked by far less poverty and hardship. America, however, is not all a land of milk and honey, as **Johann Dietel**, the youngest son of a peasant family from Kleinlosnitz in Upper Franconia, who, in 1848, at the age of 18 emigrated to Oswego, Iowa, with his sister Margaretha, wrote in letters to his family back home: "If you want to get anywhere in America you must work hard." And in another letter: "A scalawag is just as worthless here too!" Johann Dietel belonged to a group of 30 people who emigrated together from the area near Münchberg in the Fichtel Mountains. Undoubtedly an unforgettable image, the day when a total of 30 people abandoned the tiny rural village, never to return! They were not going away for just a little while, they were leaving for good. The group walked and traveled by carriage as far as Einbeck. In a letter to his folks, Johann advises his older brother, who left his hometown later, together with the remaining brothers and sisters, to "take the train"! Having arrived in Oswego, the older brother described the distance from Kleinlosnitz to Oswego in hours: "It took us 173 hours to travel from Kleinlosnitz to Bremerhaven, then 2,200 hours to cross the Atlantic to New York, another 680 hours from New York to Oswego, adding up to a total of 3,053 German hours." Despite their using the train for a portion of their journey, the entire trip took a good three months! Other sources refer to elder brother Johann Konrad Dietel's trip to Oswego having lasted two months. One year later, this very brother, who never felt at home in America, decided to embark on the same lengthy journey again, this time returning to Germany.

Von Kleinlosnitz nach Bremerhaven sind es 173, von da an über das atlantische Meer bis New York 2200, von da bis Oswego 680 Stunden, im ganzen 3053 deutsche Stunden. / It took us 173 hours to travel from Kleinlosnitz to Bremerhaven, then 2,200 hours to cross the Atlantic to New York, another 680 hours from New York to Oswego, adding up to a total of 3,053 German hours.

Helene Maeckel konnte noch nicht schreiben, als sie 1852 mit ihrer Familie aus Lengefeld im sächsischen Reifland auswanderte. Sie war zwei Jahre

Sammlung Deutsches Auswandererhaus / Collection German Emigration Center

Helene Maeckel

***11.01.1850 Lengefeld (heute / today: Sachsen / Saxony);**

†1937 Texas, USA

Als 2-jährige wanderte Helene Maeckel 1852 mit ihrer Familie nach Texas aus. Zwei ihrer drei Brüder starben während der Atlantiküberfahrt.

Helene Maeckel was just two years old when she immigrated to Texas with her family. Two of her three brothers died on the transatlantic crossing.

alt. Die Passagierliste der Bremer Bark „Juno" verzeichnet ihren Vater: „J.G. Mäckel mit Fam. 6 Personen".
Der Huf- und Waffenschmied wollte seinen erlernten Beruf weiter ausüben, in Deutschland wurde er nicht mehr gebraucht. In Frelsburg in Texas könnten Schmiede gebraucht werden, hatte ihm ein befreundeter Schmied geschrieben. Ein kleines Kind kann die Tragödie, die jetzt beginnt, wohl kaum beschreiben. Die Nachfahren können nur die Fakten überliefern.
Auf der stürmischen Überfahrt sterben zwei ihrer Brüder. Ein Jahr nach der Ankunft in Frelsburg stirbt ihre Mutter an Gelbfieber, eine Krankheit, der im 19. Jahrhundert viele zum Opfer fielen, die auch ihren Vater drei Jahre später dahinrafft. Sie ist sechs Jahre alt und mutterseelenallein im Land der Träume ihrer Eltern. Ein Onkel nimmt sich des kleinen Mädchens an. Sie heiratet mit 18 Jahren einen Kaufmann in Shelby in Texas und bringt acht Kinder zur Welt: Otilia, Johanna, Agnes, Ida, Dorothea, Arthur, Walter Charles und Annie.

Justina Tubbe aus Oderberg in Brandenburg, war die Witwe eines Webers und Mutter von acht Kindern.
Justina Tubbe from Oderberg in Brandenburg, widow of a weaver, gave birth to eight children.

Damit es den Kindern einmal besser geht, dafür nehmen viele Mütter große Strapazen auf sich. **Justina Tubbe** aus Oderberg in Brandenburg war die Witwe eines Webers und Mutter von neun Kindern. Hungersnöte, Missern-

Helene Maeckel was still too little to read and write when she emigrated with her family from the town of Lengefeld in the Saxon region of Reifland in 1852. The passenger manifest from the barque *Juno*, registered in Bremen, lists her father as "J. G. Maeckel and family of 6." There wasn't enough work in Germany for the trained blacksmith and armorer to feed his family, and so he decided to move to Frelsburg in Texas where men of his trade were in demand, as a blacksmith friend had written him. A small child can hardly begin to relate the tragedy which began to evolve; her descendants have passed down the facts.
Two of Helene Maeckel's brothers died during the stormy ocean crossing. One year following the family's arrival in Frelsburg, her mother fell victim to and died of yellow fever, a disease which killed countless numbers in the 19th century. Three years later, her father also died of yellow fever. Helene, now age six, was all alone in the land of her parents' dreams. Fortunately, her uncle took her in. At the age of 18, Helene Maeckel married a merchant from Shelby, Texas, and gave birth to eight children: Otilia, Johanna, Agnes, Ida, Dorothea, Arthur, Walter Charles and Annie.

A mother will go to almost any length to ensure that her children get off to a good start in life. **Justina Tubbe** from Oderberg in Brandenburg was no exception. Famine, crop failures, and high taxes overshadowed the prospects for any kind of future for Justina Tubbe, widow of a weaver, and her nine children. Her eldest son, Wilhelm, and his sister, Charlotte, left Germany for Texas in 1852. By selling her house, and living in it as a paying tenant, Justina Tubbe scraped just enough money together to

Gisela Laudi

Justina Tubbe

*29.05.1795, Bad Freienwalde, Preußen (heute / today: Brandenburg);
†um / about 1869 Texas, USA

Ein Foto von Justina Tubbe existiert nicht. Dieses Aquarell hat die Nachfahrin Gisela Laudi gemalt. / No photo of Justina Tubbe exists. This water-color portrait was painted by Gisela Laudi, a descendant of Justina Tubbe's.

ten, hohe Steuern verdüsterten die Zukunftsaussichten. 1852 wanderte ihr ältester Sohn Wilhelm mit seiner Schwester Charlotte nach Texas aus. Die Überfahrt und ein kleines Kapital für einen Neubeginn in Amerika hatte Justina Tubbe durch den Verkauf ihres Hauses, in dem sie dann zur Miete wohnte, ermöglicht. Als sie sah, dass es für ihre beiden bei ihr gebliebenen Söhne keine Zukunftsperspektiven gab, folgte sie dem Drängen ihrer Kinder und fasste 1855 den Entschluss auszuwandern. Justina Tubbe war 60, ihr jüngster Sohn August 14 Jahre alt, als sie nach Nacogdoches in Texas auswanderten.

In einer Familienchronik danken die Nachfahren Justina Tubbe für ihr Vorbild: „Hunderte von Tubbes haben ihre Wurzeln bei Justina. Ihr Beispiel an Mut hat vielen ihrer Nachkommen geholfen, furchtlos neue Wege zur Lösung von Problemen, Konflikten und Schicksalsschlägen zu suchen. Welches Beispiel war die Tubbe Familie für den ‚Großen Amerikanischen Traum'."

Fast könnte man glauben, die Straßen von New York seien tatsächlich mit Gold gepflastert, dass man ständig auf Ölquellen stößt und dass jeder Tellerwäscher Millionär werden kann, wenn man die Geschichten der ausgewanderten Erfinder und Glückspilze liest. Wie ein Märchen klingt die Geschichte des Schneiders **Paul Lemke**. Zuversichtlich und abenteuerlustig zieht es den 1851 in Soldin in Brandenburg geborenen Gesellen auf seinen Wanderjahren schon bis nach London. Mit 23 Jahren wagt der tapfere Schneider

Sammlung Deutsches Auswandererhaus / Collection German Emigration Center

Paul Lemke

***20.11.1851 Soldin, Preußen (heute / today: Myslibórz, Polen / Poland); †11.02.1908 Hawaii (heute / today: USA)**

Der Schneider aus Soldin wurde 1881 in Hawaii zum königlichen Hofschneider ernannt. / The tailor from Soldin was appointed tailor to the royal court of Hawaii in 1881.

purchase their passages and provide them with a meagre amount of capital to get started in the New World. She soon realized the lack of perspective for the two sons who had remained behind in Germany, thus giving in to her children's urging and emigrating with the rest of the family in 1855. By now, Justina Tubbe was 60 years old and her youngest son August 14 years old when the rest of the family set out for Nacogdoches, Texas.

The family chronicle reflects the gratitude Justina Tubbe's descendants feel and the pride they take in the example she set: "Hundreds of Tubbes are rooted in Justina. Her courage served as an example to numerous descendants to look for the solution to problems, conflicts and strokes of fate by going one's own way. The Tubbe family embodied a fine example of the 'great American dream'."

On hearing the stories of the men and women who forged new paths encountering luck along the way, one is indeed tempted to believe that the streets of New York were paved with gold, oil wells lingered around every corner and that virtually everyone struck it rich.

The story of the tailor **Paul Lemke** resembles a fairy tale, too. Born in Soldin in Brandenburg in 1851, the young and confident journeyman tailor ventured as far as London during his years of apprenticeship travel. The daring young man decided to go to America at the age of 23, working first in New York, then in Passaic, New Jersey, before returning back home to Germany where he met his cousin, Agnes Graumann. Despite their brief courtship, Paul Lemke set out for the New World once again, this time for Honolulu, Hawaii. It just so happened that the King of Hawaii had a great weakness for Prussian military uniforms and ceremony. In fact, the bandleader of the Hawaiian military band was a Prussian and the king now desired nothing more than to see the royal band in Prussian

Ottmar Mergenthaler

***11.05.1854 Hachtel, Schwaben (heute / today: Baden-Württemberg); †28.10.1899 Baltimore, Maryland, USA**

Der Erfinder der „Linotype" wanderte mit 18 Jahren nach Amerika aus.
The inventor of the *Linotype* immigrated to America at the age of 18.

den Sprung nach Amerika. Er schneidert in New York, in Passaic in New Jersey, dann kehrt er für einige Jahre nach Hause zurück, lernt seine Cousine Agnes Graumann kennen, bricht trotzdem wieder auf in die Neue Welt und landet in Honolulu auf Hawaii. Das Glück will, dass der König von Hawaii ein Faible für preußisches Militärzeremoniell hat. Die hawaiianische Militärkapelle wird bereits von einem preußischen Kapellmeister geleitet, nun will er seine Hofkapelle in preußischen Uniformen sehen. Seine Wahl fällt auf Paul Lemke. So wird der Schneider aus Soldin im Jahre 1881 zum königlichen Hofschneider von Hawaii. Nun fehlt ihm zu seinem Glück nur noch eine Frau. Er fährt nach Hause, hält um die Hand von Agnes Graumann an, die nach zehn Jahren noch immer ledig ist, und sie gehen 1886 gemeinsam nach Honolulu.

Ottmar Mergenthaler kam 1854 im schwäbischen Dorf Hachtel zur Welt und war zum Erfinder geboren. Mit elf Jahren repariert er die Kirchturmuhr. Mit 18 Jahren wandert er aus und revolutioniert von Amerika aus das Druckgewerbe. Er erfindet eine besondere Form der mechanischen Bleisatzmaschine, die „Linotype", die weltweit exportiert wird.

Auch Hollywood musste erst erfunden werden. Die amerikanische Traumfabrik wird gegründet von dem deutschen Aus-

Auch Hollywood musste erst erfunden werden. Die amerikanische Traumfabrik wird gegründet von dem deutschen Auswanderer Carl Laemmle aus Laupheim in Oberschwaben. / Hollywood had not yet been invented, that is until the German emigrant Carl Laemmle from Laupheim in Upper Swabia moved to America and founded the U.S. dream factory.

uniforms. He chose Paul Lemke for the job. Thus, the tailor from Soldin advanced to royal court tailor of Hawaii in 1881. All he lacked to make his happiness complete was a wife. Lemke travelled back home, asked for Agnes Graumann's hand in marriage, who in spite of the ten-year interval had not married, and the couple set out for Honolulu in the year 1886.

Ottmar Mergenthaler, born in the Swabian village of Hachtel in 1854, was born to be an inventor. At the tender age of 11, he repaired the clock on the church spire, and at the age of 18 he decided to emigrate to America where he revolutionized the printing industry with a new mechanical typesetting machine, the *Linotype*, which was soon exported all over the world.

Hollywood had not yet been invented, that is until the German emigrant **Carl Laemmle** from Laupheim in Upper Swabia moved to America and founded the U.S. dream factory. Carl Laemmle, born in 1867, was the tenth of 13 children born to a Jewish family who lived a very humble life. Carl's father borrowed money to give his son on his 17th birthday so the latter could buy a passage to New York. Once in the New World, the young man first worked as a messenger boy, and this is where the fairy tale begins. Eager to locate his brother whose address he did not know, Carl placed an ad in a Chicago newspaper. The publisher of the German-language Chicago paper *Illinois Staats Zeitung*, whose secretary was none other than Carl's brother Joseph, noticed the ad and immediately forwarded a train ticket and money to Carl in New York. In Chicago, Carl Laemmle started out again as a

wanderer **Carl Laemmle** aus Laupheim in Oberschwaben.
Carl Laemmle, geboren 1867, war das zehnte Kind unter den 13 Geschwistern einer in bescheidenen Verhältnissen lebenden jüdischen Familie. Zu seinem 17. Geburtstag schenkt ihm sein Vater mit geliehenem Geld eine Schiffspassage nach New York. Dort arbeitet er als Laufbursche und jetzt fängt das Märchen an: Er sucht seinen Bruder, dessen Adresse ihm unbekannt ist, und gibt eine Anzeige in der Zeitung auf. Tatsächlich erreicht sein Brief den Herausgeber der Chicagoer „Illinois Staats Zeitung", dessen Sekretär niemand anderes ist als Carls Bruder Joseph, der umgehend ein Bahnticket und Geld nach New York schickt. Wieder arbeitet er als Laufbursche, dann als Buchhalter und später als Manager eines Bekleidungsgeschäfts. 1906 kauft er sein erstes Kino.
Im Jahr 1912 gründet er die „Universal Film Manufacturing Company". 1913 beginnt er bei Los Angeles eine Filmfabrik aufzubauen: die „Universal City Studios". HOLLYWOOD! 1930 findet die Weltpremiere der ersten Filmproduktion seines Sohnes Carl Laemmle Jr. statt: „All Quiet on the Western Front" („Im Westen nichts Neues").

Museum zur Geschichte von Christen und Juden auf Schloss Großlaupheim

Carl Laemmle

***17.01.1867 Laupheim, Schwaben (heute / today: Baden-Württemberg); †24.09.1939 Beverly Hills, California, USA**

Der Gründer Hollywoods bürgte während des Nationalsozialismus u.a. für Hertha Nathorff. / The man who created Hollywood vouched for example for Hertha Nathorff who fled Germany during the National Socialism.

messenger boy, went on to become a bookkeeper and finally became the manager of a clothing store. In 1906, he bought his first movie theater.
Laemmle formed the *Universal Film Manufacturing Company* in 1912. One year later, in 1913, he began setting up the *Universal City Studios* in Los Angeles. HOLLYWOOD! The world premiere of his son Carl Laemmle Jr.'s first motion picture production, *All Quiet on the Western Front*, took place in 1930. Up until his death in 1939, Carl Laemmle vouched for more than 300 Jews seeking refuge from Nazi Germany in the United States.

However, the 20th century is not the age of fairy tales. Immigration regulations in the United States were tightened considerably, making the decision to start a new life in the New World just as difficult and courageous as it had been in previous centuries. At the same time, those interested in making America their new home had access to more information than in years before. The stories of domestic help and parlor maids in the U.S.A. tend to still somewhat resemble fairy tales. These women dreamed of a better life for themselves and made their dreams come true. Hollywood movies usually have a happy end (or, at least, they used to), and such is the case with **Martha Huener**, originally from Bremerhaven.
Martha Huener had to persuade her father to let her emigrate. She required his permission as she was only 17 years old at the time. Her aunts in America assured her of wonderful opportunities, vouched for her and paid her passage, which was a far cry from the transatlantic crossing most emigrants had made in steerage class on sailing ships. Martha Huener wrote that she had never before laid eyes on such luxury. Her aunt Kaethe was at the pier to pick her up on her arrival in New York on December 20, 1923. On the drive home through Manhattan, Martha was rendered speechless by the city all decked out in Christmas décor. Within nine years' time Martha had married and opened a baked goods shop with her husband in New Jersey.

Während der Zeit des Nationalsozialismus verhilft Carl Laemmle bis zu seinem Tod 1939 mehr als 300 Juden zur Auswanderung, indem er Bürgschaften übernimmt.

Sammlung Deutsches Auswandererhaus / Collection German Emigration Center

Martha Hüner

*** 01.07.1906 Geestemünde, Preußen (heute / today: Bremen);**
† 03.07.1987 Bremerhaven, Bremen, Deutschland / Germany

Die 17-jährige Martha Hüner kurz vor ihrer Auswanderung 1923.
The 17-year-old Martha Huener shortly before emigrating in 1923.

Im 20. Jahrhundert lassen sich die Geschichten nicht mehr als Märchen erzählen. Auch waren die Aufnahmebedingungen für die Einwanderung erheblich erschwert worden. Der Entschluss, ein neues Leben zu gründen, zeugt von demselben Mut wie in den Zeiten vorher. Aber jeder, der auswandern wollte, konnte mehr über das Land seiner Träume wissen, so ganz ins Ungewisse musste sich keiner mehr aufmachen. In den Geschichten der Haushaltsgehilfinnen und Dienstmädchen hängt noch ein Rest von Märchen. Sie träumten von einem besseren Leben und folgten ihren Träumen. Mit einem Happy End müssen die Filme aus Hollywood enden, bei **Martha Hüner** aus Bremerhaven trifft es ein: Sie musste ihren Vater überreden, sie auswandern zu lassen. Sie brauchte seine Erlaubnis, denn sie war erst 17 Jahre alt. Ihre Tanten in Amerika versprachen ihr sehr gute Aussichten, bürgten für sie und bezahlten ihre Reise, die anders aussah als eine Überfahrt im Zwischendeck eines Dampfschiffes. So viel Luxus habe sie noch nie gesehen, schrieb sie nach Hause. Als sie am 10. Dezember 1923 in New York eintrifft, holt ihre Tante Käthe sie ab und sie fährt durch das weihnachtlich geschmückte New York. Neun Jahre später ist sie verheiratet und eröffnet mit ihrem Mann eine Bäckerei in New Jersey.

Ob diese Geschichte wirklich ein Happy End hat, wissen wir nicht. Wir wüssten gar nichts von **Alzbeta K.**, hätte nicht eine Angestellte der amerikanischen Einwanderungsbehörde auf Ellis Island Buch geführt über ihre Eindrücke von den

Whether or not the following tale had a happy end is uncertain. Had it not been for one of the women working as an immigration official who kept a journal of her impressions of the immigrants we would not know a thing about **Alzbeta K.** The immigration inspector was utterly surprised when, in 1927, she saw this young woman, babe in arms, apply for re-entry to the U.S. after having left a short time earlier. Alzbeta K. was 30 years old when she packed up to move to the United States for the first time, in 1921. A bold decision at the time, for apparently she knew no one at all in the New World and there was no one to vouch for her. The inspector reviewing Alzbeta's case in 1927 felt that the Immigration Authorities had evidently been very lackadaisical on approving her entrance to the country the first time, in 1921. The infant she was carrying was the son of Edward K., her employer, whom she had worked for after her first arrival, and therefore, an American citizen. On becoming pregnant, Edward K.'s mother had prevented their marriage, assuming this had been a premeditated move on Alzbeta's part. Alzbeta returned home to what is now the Czech Republic, then part of the Austro-Hungarian Empire, and her mother. Edward K., father of the baby and Alzbeta's employer, implored her to return to America, which she did, landing at Ellis Island in December 1927. There is no record of what happened to Alzbeta after this…

No matter who or when, each immigrant's story is a personal story, the story of an individual life. And each life touches many others. As time passes, living conditions have changed, technological advances have been made, all of which have affected and altered the way in which the stories of many lives evolve. While the personal motives for migration remain the same—scarce perspectives for the future in the country of origin, loss of family members, loss of income or financial means,

Einwanderern. Sie staunte nicht schlecht, als 1927 eine Frau mit einem Säugling im Arm vor ihr steht, die kurz vorher ausgereist war und nun zum zweiten Mal einwandern will. Alzbeta K. war schon 30 Jahre alt, als sie ihren Koffer packte und 1921 zum ersten Mal nach Amerika auswanderte. Ein kühner Entschluss, denn sie schien in dem fremden Land niemanden zu kennen und eine angekündigte Bürgschaft blieb aus. Wie lasch offenbar die Einreisebehörde ihrer Arbeit nachging, darüber mokiert sich die Beamtin, denn sie versteht nicht, auf welche Weise Alzbeta 1921 überhaupt ins Land kommen konnte. Der Säugling in ihrem Arm ist der Sohn von Edward K., ihrem Dienstherrn, bei dem sie nach ihrer ersten Ankunft als Dienstmädchen gearbeitet hatte, ein kleiner amerikanischer Staatsbürger. Als sie schwanger war, verbot Edwards Mutter die Heirat, weil sie Alzbeta kalte Berechnung unterstellte. Alzbeta ging mit ihrem Kind zurück zu ihrer Mutter nach Tschechien, das damals ein Teil der Donaumonarchie war. Der Vater des Kindes und Dienstherr Edward K. bat sie aber, mit seinem Sohn zurückzukommen. So steht sie im Dezember 1927 wieder in Ellis Island. Hier verliert sich ihre Spur...

Die Geschichte jedes Einwanderers zu jeder Zeit ist eine ganze Lebensgeschichte, ein ganzes Leben. Und wie jedes Leben betrifft ein einzelnes viele andere Leben. Mit dem Fortschreiten der Zeit ändert sich die Form, diese Lebensgeschichten zu erzählen. Mit dem Fortschritt der Technologien verändern sich die Bedingungen der Auswande-

Sammlung Deutsches Auswandererhaus / Collection German Emigration Center

destruction on a material and mental level—the First and Second World Wars of the 20th century created a different type of plight. Although transatlantic crossings now only took a week or two as compared to months in a bygone era, and objectives had become more calculable and perceptible, the decision to abandon one's country and mother tongue is nevertheless a test of personal courage. Facing new living conditions perhaps causes a smaller degree of anxiety; the decision to emigrate is perhaps not quite so threatening or venturesome. But each and every individual is painfully aware of the fears and anxieties linked to this one great adventure and the need to succeed.

Richard Morgner's story, as chronicled by his daughter Evelyn in 2002, is a modern tale of success, a tale of family pride, but with a near-fateful end. As a young man growing up in Wesermünde (today a part of Bremerhaven), Richard Morgner was supposed to take over his grandfather's guesthouse, which is why he had completed an apprenticeship as a waiter. The family home, including the guesthouse, was destroyed in an air raid in 1944. Unable to cope with the loss, first Morgner's grandfather committed suicide, then his father three years later. Richard Morgner apprenticed as a baker and found a job. He then met his future wife, Eleonore Holz, and both began to take interest in the "American way of life." In 1954, the couple set out for the United States; among their belongings was a sealed porcelain bowl of soil from their hometown, Bremerhaven. Richard Morgner soon got a job as a welder for the Geis Steel Works. Ten years later, he had become a partner in the company. "Now that they had two companies, three new company cars and properties in Virginia and D.C. they, 'felt in heaven,' 'sitting like big shots' smoking

Richard Morgner

*** 28.10.1926 Wesermünde, Preußen (heute / today: Bremen); † 13.08.1999 USA**

Richard Morgner und seine Frau Eleonore erreichen am 5. Mai 1954 den Hafen von New York auf der „Olympia". / Richard Morgner and his wife Eleonore arrived in the port of New York on the *Olympia* on May 5, 1954.

rung, die Lebensbedingungen überhaupt. Die Notlagen des 20. Jahrhunderts haben durch den Ersten und Zweiten Weltkrieg äußerlich ein anderes Gesicht bekommen, die inneren Beweggründe sind die gleichen: geringe Zukunftsperspektiven im eigenen Land, Verlust von Familienangehörigen, Verlust des Vermögens, materielle und seelische Zerstörung. Auch wenn die Überfahrten nicht mehr Wochen und Monate dauern, die Ziele berechenbarer und deutlicher vor Augen stehen, ist der Entschluss, das Land, in dem man groß geworden ist, dessen Sprache man spricht, zu verlassen, immer eine Mutprobe. Vielleicht sind die Ängste vor den neuen Lebensbedingungen rein äußerlich weniger groß, der Aufbruch nicht ganz so ungewiss und abenteuerlich. Für jeden Einzelnen bleibt es das große Abenteuer, das es zu bestehen gilt.

Und aus einem Märchen oder einer Dienstmädchenkolportage wird eine moderne Erfolgsstory, wie die von **Richard Morgner**, die seine Tochter Evelyn 2002 aufgeschrieben hat. Eine Geschichte voller Familienstolz, aber mit fast schicksalhaftem Ende. Richard Morgner sollte als junger Mann in Wesermünde (heute ein Teil von Bremerhaven) das Gasthaus seines Großvaters übernehmen und hatte dafür eine Kellnerlehre gemacht. 1944 wurde das Haus der Familie, in dem sich das Gasthaus befand, bei einem Bombenangriff vollständig zerstört. Der Großvater nahm sich das Leben. Sein Vater verkraftete die Verluste nicht und nahm sich dreieinhalb Jahre später auch das Leben. Richard Morgner machte eine Bäckerlehre und bekam eine Anstellung. Er lernte seine spätere Frau Eleonore Holz kennen und beide begannen sich für Amerika zu interessieren, für den „American Way of Life". 1954 brachen sie auf, im Gepäck ein versiegelter Porzellantopf mit Erde aus Bremerhaven. Richard Morgner wurde Schweißer bei den Geis-Stahlwerken. Zehn Jahre später war er bereits Teilhaber der Werke. „Nun, da sie zwei Firmen, drei neue Firmenautos und Land hatten, fühlten sie sich wie im Himmel sitzend und Zigarre rauchend wie die Bonzen (...).

1954 brachen sie auf, im Gepäck ein versiegelter Porzellantopf mit Erde aus Bremerhaven. / In 1954, the couple set out for the United States; among their belongings was a sealed porcelain bowl of soil from their hometown, Bremerhaven.

the cigars Neil bought for them (...) In total, Opa set up or co-founded thirteen companies in his career plus several real estate partnerships with his partners (...)." Then the turning point in this wonderful story: "Opa always had an interest in flying and in 1971 he decided to learn how to fly (...). Later, in 1984, Opa bought a *Cessna Centurion* (Cessna 210), the plane in which he and Omi were killed 15 years later (...). Over a six-year period, from the end of 1991 to early 1998, Omi and Opa told me stories of their lives directly and then in the summer and autumn of 2002 told me their stories posthumously via the recorded tapes, as they wanted you, their adored grandchildren, to understand more about their lives and histories before your arrival (...)." (Evelyn Morgner, 2002)

The land of infinite opportunity is defined by an enormous variety of nationalities, traditions and customs, and one cannot expect immigrants to assimilate at once. Over a period of three generations **Mildred Lange-Ranzini**'s family created a variegated story as American as apple pie. Her parents never told her much about Germany. There are no stories to tell if parents do not pass them on to their children. Consequently, Mildred Lange-Ranzini does not know why her parents emigrated to the United States for the second time after getting married.
Mildred Lange-Ranzini is the daughter of Martha Elise Hintze and Henry Lange, both of whom originally came from northern Germany and emigrated to the United States by way of New York in 1923. They met at the *German Social Club* in New York, married in Germany in 1928, then returned to the U.S. where Henry Lange established a delicatessen shop and the couple raised five children.
Daughter Mildred married an Italian man named Ranzini,

Am Ende seiner Karriere hatte Opa dreizehn Firmen gegründet oder mitgegründet." Diese glückliche Geschichte bekommt eine schicksalhafte Wendung: „Opa hatte immer Interesse am Fliegen. 1971 beschloss er, selbst zu fliegen. 1984 kaufte Opa eine „Cessna Centurion" (Cessna 210), das Flugzeug, in dem er und Omi 15 Jahre später starben (...). Von Ende 1991 bis Anfang 1998 erzählten mir Omi und Opa ihre Lebensgeschichte. Sie wollten für Euch, ihre geliebten Enkelkinder, ihr Leben, ihre Erlebnisse aus der Zeit vor Eurer Ankunft verständlich machen (...)." (Evelyn Morgner, 2002).

Im Land der unbegrenzten Möglichkeiten kann nicht Assimilation von Einwanderern gefordert werden. Eine Vielzahl von Nationalitäten, Traditionen und Bräuchen definiert das Land. In drei Generationen erhält die Familie von **Mildred Lange-Ranzini** eine amerikanische und eigene, bunte Geschichte. Aus Deutschland haben ihre Eltern wenig erzählt. Es gibt keine Geschichten zu berichten, wenn die Eltern sie nicht erzählt haben. Und so bleiben die Gründe, weshalb ihre Eltern nach ihrer Hochzeit zum zweiten Mal in die USA ausgewandert sind, im Dunkeln.

Mildred Lange-Ranzini ist die Tochter von Martha Elise Hintze und Henry Lange, die beide 1923 aus Norddeutschland nach New York ausgewandert sind. Sie lernten sich in New York im „German Social Club" kennen, heirateten 1928 in Deutschland und kehrten wieder in die USA zurück. Henry Lange gründete ein Delikatessengeschäft. Das Paar bekam fünf Kinder. Tochter Mildred heiratete wiederum den Italiener Ranzini und lebt in New Jersey. Ihre Tochter Angela heiratete einen Amerikaner chinesischer Herkunft. Angelas Töchter können auswählen, für welchen Strang ihrer Herkunft sie sich interessieren wollen. Für ein Rechercheprojekt der Schule über

Trotzdem ist für Großmutter Mildred Lange-Ranzini noch immer Weihnachten ohne deutsche Weihnachtsplätzchen nicht Weihnachten. / Be that as it may, Christmas is not Christmas to grandmother Mildred Lange-Ranzini without homemade German Christmas cookies.

cine plus

Mildred Lange-Ranzini und ihre Tochter Angela mit Familie in Belle Mead, New Jersey, USA. Die Familie Lange-Ranzini hat ihre Wurzeln in Italien, Deutschland und China. / Mildred Lange-Ranzini and her daughter Angela with her family in Belle Mead, New Jersey, U.S.A. The Lange-Ranzini family has roots in Italy, Germany and China.

and they settled in New Jersey. Her daughter Angela married an American of Chinese origin. Angela's daughters, in turn, can choose which side of their ancestry they find most appealing. During a research project on ethnic origin at school, both daughters opted for Germany. Why not Italy, or China? The answer is simple—half the class had already chosen China. Perhaps the parents' favorite foods reveal their backgrounds: Mildred's daughter Angela loves potatoes, Angela's husband loves rice, one daughter loves potatoes while the other prefers pasta and rice. Be that as it may, Christmas is not Christmas to grandmother Mildred Lange-Ranzini without homemade German Christmas cookies.

The Nazi regime forced political dissidents and Jews to flee the country. Happy were those who had the financial means to leave their native country and succeeded in emigrating.

Erich Koch-Weser, born in Bremerhaven in 1875, both a lawyer and politician, was a staunch Democrat. In 1933, the Nazis revoked the accreditation of the lawyer and notary Koch-Weser, a man who had been elected mayor of three towns in Germany, Minister of the Interior from 1919 to 1921,

ihre ethnische Abstammung wählten sie Deutschland. Warum nicht Italien, warum nicht China? Sie antworteten, weil die Hälfte der Klasse China gewählt hatte. Höchstens das Lieblingsessen kann vielleicht etwas über kulturelle Vorlieben erzählen: Angela, Mildreds Tochter, mag am liebsten Kartoffeln, ihr Mann Reis, eine Tochter mag Kartoffeln, die andere Nudeln und Reis. Trotzdem ist für Großmutter Mildred Lange-Ranzini noch immer Weihnachten ohne deutsche Weihnachtsplätzchen nicht Weihnachten.

als Reichsminister und Vizekanzler in Berlin

Sammlung Deutsches Auswandererhaus / Collection German Emigration Center

Der Nationalsozialismus zwang vor allem politisch Andersdenkende und Juden zur Auswanderung. Glücklich war, wem sie überhaupt gelang, wer die Mittel dafür hatte oder auftreiben konnte.

Der Anwalt und Politiker **Erich Koch-Weser** war überzeugter Demokrat. 1933 entziehen die Nationalsozialisten dem 1875 in Bremerhaven geborenen Bürgermeister von drei Städten, dem Innenminister von 1919 bis 1921, dem Vizekanzler und Justizminister der Weimarer Republik die Zulassung als Rechtsanwalt und Notar, weil seine Mutter Jüdin war. Gleichzeitig wird er wegen seiner politischen Überzeugung verfolgt. Zehn Monate nach dem Machtantritt Hitlers geht Erich Koch-Weser mit seiner Frau und zwei kleinen Söhnen ins Exil nach Brasilien.

Erich Koch-Weser

***26.02.1875 Bremerhaven (heute / today: Bremen); †19.10.1944 Brasilien / Brazil**

Der Politiker und überzeugte Demokrat verließ das nationalsozialistische Deutschland im November 1933 auf der „Madrid". / The politician and staunch Democrat left Nazi Germany on board the *Madrid* in November 1933.

Vice-Chancellor and Minister of Justice during the Weimar Republic, for the simple reason that his mother was of Jewish extraction. He was also persecuted because of his political conviction. Two months after Hitler's rise to power Erich Koch-Weser left Germany with his wife and two sons to live in exile in Brazil.

Hertha Nathorff, née Einstein, and her husband, Erich Nathorff, both phyisicians, were stripped of their authorization to practice medicine in 1933. In the course of the November pogroms of 1938, Erich Nathorff was carried off to the concentration camp Sachsenhausen, then released five weeks later. Although Carl Laemmle, founder of Hollywood, vouched for the couple, the U.S. Consulate refused to issue the required visas. Finally, in order to ensure their son's safety, they sent him to England on one of the children's transports. The Nathorffs emigrated to England in 1939 and finally received their visas for the U.S. in 1940, when they left Europe for New York.

Immer fand ich den Namen falsch, den man uns gab: Emigranten. / Das heißt doch Auswanderer. Aber wir / Wanderten doch nicht aus, nach freiem Entschluss / Wählend ein andres Land. Wanderten wir doch auch nicht / Ein in ein Land, dort zu bleiben, womöglich für immer. / Sondern wir flohen. Vertriebene sind wir, Verbannte... I always felt the name they gave us was wrong: emigrants. That means leaving a country. And yet we didn't leave of our own free will, choosing another country instead. Nor did we enter a country to stay there, perhaps for all time. Instead, we fled. We were displaced, banished...

Aus: / Freely adapted from: Bertolt Brecht: „Über die Bezeichnung Emigranten", 1937.

Die Deutsche Bibliothek, Deutsches Exilarchiv 1933–1945, Frankfurt am Main

Hertha Nathorff

*** 01.06.1895 Laupheim, Schwaben (heute / today: Baden-Württemberg);**
† 10.06.1993 New York, New York, USA

Gerade hatte das Ehepaar den mühsamen Aufbau einer neuen Existenz in den USA geschafft, starb Erich Nathorff 1954 an den Folgen seiner KZ-Inhaftierung.
The Nathorffs struggled to build a new life in the United States. Erich Nathorff passed away in 1954 due to complications rooted in his imprisonment in a concentration camp.

Der Ärztin **Hertha Nathorff**, geb. Einstein, und ihrem Mann, dem Arzt Erich Nathorff, wird 1933 die Kassenzulassung entzogen. Erich Nathorff wird im Zuge der Novemberpogrome 1938 ins Konzentrationslager Sachsenhausen verschleppt. Nach fünf Wochen wird er wieder freigelassen. Trotz der Bürgschaft von Carl Laemmle, dem Gründer Hollywoods, stellt das amerikanische Konsulat die notwendigen Visa nicht aus. Ihr Sohn wird mit einem der „Kindertransporte" nach England geschickt. 1939 emigriert das Ehepaar Nathorff ebenfalls nach England. 1940 erhalten sie gemeinsam ihre Visa für die Einreise in die USA. Sie emigrieren nach New York.

Hannah Levinsky-Koevary lebt heute in Jerusalem. Sie war zehn Monate alt, als ihre Eltern im April 1949 in die USA emigrierten. Ihre Eltern, polnische Juden, hatten sich in einem Konzentrationslager kennen gelernt. Beide haben den Holocaust überlebt. In einem Lager im bayrischen Landsberg, wohin Displaced Persons, aus ihrer Heimat vertriebene und verschleppte Menschen, nach Kriegsende gebracht wurden, trafen sie sich wieder. Die einzige noch lebende Verwandte, die Schwester ihrer Mutter, lebte in den USA. Zu ihr nach New York flüchtete sich das Paar mit seiner kleinen Tochter Hannah.

Hannah Levinsky-Koevary lives in Jerusalem today. She was 10 months old when her parents emigrated to the United States in April 1949. Both mother and father were Polish Jews and had met at a concentration camp. Both survived the Holocaust. After the war was over, they meet again at a camp for Displaced Persons in Landsberg (Bavaria). The sole relative who survived the extermination camps, Hannah's aunt, her mother's sister, lived in the United States. It is this aunt where Hannah's parents found refuge with their baby daughter after emigrating to the U.S.A.

Sammlung Deutsches Auswandererhaus / Collection German Emigration Center

Hannah Levinsky-Koevary

*** 1948 Landsberg (heute / today: Bayern / Bavaria)**

Heute lebt Hannah Levinsky-Koevary mit ihrer Familie in Jerusalem, Israel.
Hannah Levinsky-Koevary lives with her family in Jerusalem, Israel today.

AUSWANDERN NACH ARGENTINIEN

EMIGRATION TO ARGENTINA

KARIN HESS

Nach Argentinien! Wer die 6.663 Seemeilen von Bremerhaven nach Buenos Aires hinter sich gebracht oder auf noch weiteren Umwegen an den Río de la Plata gelangt ist, atmet bei der Ankunft im Hafen erst einmal auf. Ist es die in greifbare Nähe gerückte Rettung vor Verfolgung, der feste Boden unter den Füßen oder der kurze Moment, bevor das Heimweh wieder übergroß wird? Die Geschichte der Auswanderung von Deutschland nach Argentinien ist außerordentlich facettenreich. Bekannt ist die Rettung jüdischer Flüchtlinge, aber auch das Untertauchen von NS-Verbrechern. Daneben gehen die "normalen" deutschen Arbeitsmigranten fast unter.

In argentinisch-deutschen Familiengeschichten nehmen romantisch verklärte Erinnerungen an die verlassene Heimat häufig einen festen Platz ein. Die Erfahrung prägt unweigerlich noch das Leben der Kinder und Kindeskinder. Wie der bekannte argentinische Dichter Jorge Luis Borges einmal über die Einwanderer in Argentinien sagte: „Wir sind alle Europäer im Exil."

„Wir sind alle Europäer im Exil."
"We are all Europeans in exile."

Das alljährlich angestimmte „Oh du Fröhliche" unter dem geschmückten Weihnachtsbaum hilft manchmal schon, die gedankliche Verbundenheit mit der alten Heimat zu bewahren. So auch bei **Lebin Weckesser**, der, wie er zu sagen pflegt, „im Leib meiner Mutter ausgewandert" ist.

To Argentina! Anybody who has traveled the 6,663 nautical miles from Bremerhaven to Buenos Aires or even farther to the Río de la Plata, breathes a sigh of relief on finally arriving in the port. Is it the tangible feeling of having escaped persecution, of standing on solid ground again, or is it that brief moment before one is once again overwhelmed by homesickness? The history of emigration from Germany to Argentina is exceedingly complex and multi-faceted. It stands for human lives that were saved, for great hopes and broken dreams, but also for criminals who saw it as a safe haven.

The romantically idealized memory of the abandoned *Heimat*, or homeland, is frequently deep-seated in the stories of Argentine-German families. Inevitably, the experience influences the lives of emigrants' children and their children. As the prominent Argentine writer and poet Jorge Luis Borges once said of immigrants to Argentina, "We are all Europeans in exile."

Singing one of the season's most traditional songs, "O du Fröhliche," when the family was gathered around the Christmas tree, did indeed help to maintain the connection with the old homeland. This was certainly the case for **Lebin Weckesser**, who used to say that he had emigrated in his mother's belly. His knowledge of his parents' *Heimat* was based on the stories they told. But where was that home-

Die Heimat seiner Eltern kennt er jedoch nur aus Erzählungen. Doch wo ist diese Heimat? Für Lebins Familie war es Deutschland, obwohl sie dort nur wenige Jahre gelebt hat. Die Familiengeschichte der Weckessers ist eine Geschichte der Wanderungen. Argentinien bildet dabei den vorläufigen Schlusspunkt. Mit ihren acht Kindern lebten die Eltern bis 1921 in der Nähe von Saratov an der Wolga. In Russland gehörten sie zu den sogenannten Wolgadeutschen-Nachfahren deutscher Siedler, die sich im 18. Jahrhundert in der Region niederließen. Im deutschen Sprachgebrauch findet man für diese Nachfahren heute zumeist die Bezeichnung „Russlanddeutsche". Der Fortzug der Weckessers hatte politische Ursachen. Die Oktoberrevolution 1917 und die Machtergreifung der Bolschewiki stellten für Gegner des Kommunismus, zu denen auch die Weckessers zählten, eine Gefahr für Leib und Leben dar. Das Verlassen des Landes erwies sich häufig als der einzige Ausweg. Ein langer und beschwerlicher Weg führte sie nach Deutschland, wo sie eine kleine Landwirtschaft aufbauten. Durch bereits in Argentinien lebende Familienmitglieder ermutigt und angetrieben von der großen Hoffnung auf ein besseres Leben brach die Familie 1926 erneut auf und ging im November in Bremerhaven an Bord der „Sierra Córdoba". Wenige Wochen nach der Ankunft in der Provinz La Pampa kam Sohn Lebin auf die Welt. Trotz des mühsamen Neuanfangs in Argentinien verlor die Familie nie den Mut. Im Alter von 15 Jahren

land? For Lebin's family it was Germany although they lived there for a few years only. The story of the Weckessers is marked by migration with Argentina currently representing the last stop on a long journey. Up until 1921 the parents had lived near Saratov on the River Volga with their eight children. In Russia they were known as Volga Germans, the descendants of ethnic Germans who settled in the region during the 18th century. In present German language usage they are known as "Russian Germans." Political reasons caused the Weckesser family to leave Russia. The October Revolution of 1917 and the Bolsheviks takeover of power proved a threat to opponents of Communism and hence to the Weckesser family. Leaving the country was considered the last resort. The Weckessers set out on a long and arduous journey to Germany where they worked a small farm. Encouraged by family members already living in Argentina the family picked up and moved to Bremerhaven in 1926 where they boarded the *Sierra Córdoba* in November of the same year. Just weeks following the Weckessers' arrival in the province of La Pampa, son Lebin was born. Despite the trials and tribulations of starting out anew in Argentina the family never lost heart. At the age of 15, Lebin moved to Buenos Aires where his older brother had opened a bandoneon workshop. After an apprenticeship as a turner Lebin worked in his brother's shop for several years. Up until the Second World War bandoneons, the very soul of tango music, had been imported from Germany and were repaired in the brother's workshop where they continue to be repaired today. After 80 years, Lebin returned to Bremerhaven for the first time in 2007, the place from which his parents left their emotional *Heimat.*

Sammlung Deutsches Auswandererhaus / Collection German Emigration Center

Familie Weckesser

Passfoto der Familie Weckesser, 1926.
Passport picture of the Weckesser family, 1926.

C. Cappellari

folgte Lebin seinem älteren Bruder nach Buenos Aires, der in der Metropole eine Bandoneonwerkstatt eröffnet hatte. Im Anschluss an eine Dreherlehre unterstützte Lebin seinen Bruder für einige Jahre in der Werkstatt. Die bis zum Zweiten Weltkrieg aus Deutschland importierten Bandoneons, deren Klänge den Tango beseelen, werden in der Werkstatt bis heute repariert. Nach 80 Jahren kehrte Lebin im Jahr 2007 zum ersten Mal nach Bremerhaven zurück, an den Ort, von dem seine Eltern ihre „gefühlte" Heimat verließen.

Mit falschen Versprechungen gelockt und von einer großen Hoffnung auf ein besseres Leben besessen, zieht es in den 1920er Jahren deutsche Siedler scharenweise nach Südamerika. Die wirtschaftlich schwierige Lage in Deutschland rief besonders bei vielen jungen Leuten düstere Zukunftsvisionen hervor. In den 1920er Jahren trieben deutsche Kaufleute und Unternehmen die Urbarmachung des Binnenlandes in Argentinien durch Siedlungsprojekte voran. Was die Neuankömmlinge vorfanden, enttäuschte viele: ein ungewohntes Klima und unfruchtbare Böden. Falsche Vorstellungen und fehlende Berufserfahrung führten dazu, dass, kaum in Argentinien angekommen, eine große Zahl von Neu-Zugewanderten mit dem Rückfahrtticket in der Hand wieder an Bord in Richtung Europa ging. Wer aber waren diese hoffnungsvollen Siedler? Viele von

Lebin Weckesser

***18.01.1927 Colonia Barón, Provinz La Pampa, Argentinien / Argentina**

Für die Dreharbeiten zum Dokumentarfilm „24h Buenos Aires" kehrte Lebin Weckesser an den Ort zurück, wo seine Familie Abschied von Europa nahm: an die Columbuskaje in Bremerhaven, 2007. / For filming the documentary *24h Buenos Aires* (2007) Lebin Weckesser returned to the place where his mother bid farewell to Europe—the Columbus wharf in Bremerhaven.

Lured by hollow promises and the false hopes of a better life German emigrants flocked to South America in droves in the 1920s. The difficult economic situation in Germany at the time evoked visions of a dismal future particularly among younger men and women. In the 1920s German businessmen and companies were forging ahead with land settlement projects to cultivate interior areas of Argentina. What newcomers to the country found on their arrival, however, proved disappointing to many: an unfamiliar climate and barren land. Misconceptions and lacking professional experience caused many immigrants who had just arrived to board the next ship back to Europe, return ticket in hand. Who were these hopeful settlers? Many of them had never worked the land before and were completely overwhelmed by the new situation. Others persevered, creating lasting and influential industries. One of these was an aspiring phy-

...mit dem Rückfahrtticket in der Hand.
...return ticket in hand.

Sammlung Deutsches Auswandererhaus / Collection German Emigration Center

Johanna Ostermann

***26.04.1897 Agudo, Rio Grande do Sul, Brasilien / Brazil;**
† 20.12.1934 Colonia Liebig, Provinz Corrientes, Argentinien / Argentina

Johanna Ostermann (li.) mit ihren Schwestern Hertha und Mathilde in Brasilien, um 1902. / Johanna Ostermann (le.) with her sisters Hertha and Mathilde in Brazil, about 1902.

ihnen hatten noch nie auf dem Feld gearbeitet und waren mit der neuen Situation völlig überfordert. Andere hielten durch und schufen nachhaltige und einflussreiche Wirtschaftszweige. Eine von ihnen war die angehende Ärztin **Johanna Ostermann**, die 1925 zusammen mit ihrem Mann und 300 jungen Siedlungswilligen nach Südamerika aufbrachen. Die Überfahrt war nicht ihre erste Atlantiküberquerung. Am 26. April 1897 als Tochter eines deutschen Missionars in einem kleinen Dorf in Brasilien geboren, siedelte sich Johanna als 11-jährige mit ihrer Familie wieder in Deutschland an. 17 Jahre später sollte sie die „General Belgrano" wieder über den Atlantik, diesmal nach Paraguay bringen – dort war der Gruppe Land versprochen worden. Bei ihrer Ankunft erlitt die Kolonisationsgenossenschaft „Neu Karlsruhe" ihren ersten Schock: Das versprochene Land existierte über-

sician, **Johanna Ostermann**, who together with her husband and 300 other young adults set out for South America in 1925. The journey was not her first transatlantic crossing. As the daughter of a German missionary Johanna was born in a village in Brazil on 26 April 1897, relocating to Germany with her family as an 11-year old. Seventeen years later, on board the *General Belgrano*, she sailed across the Atlantic again, this time to Paraguay, where the group of emigrants had been promised land. On arrival the group of young adults, which had formed a colonization cooperative and planned on founding a colony named *Neu Karlsruhe*, was shocked to discover that the promised land did not even exist. Determined and persevering, they finally obtained a piece of land from the English Liebig Company, meaning that the group of immigrants had to move north to the Argentinian province of Corrientes where they were able to implement their project. A great deal of courage and hard work were needed to develop and work the land where *Colonia Liebig* was founded and still exists today. Yerba mate, the herb used to produce mate tea, the national drink of Argentina, became the number one economic factor.

Treffen von Nachfahren der Ostermanns mit deutschen Verwandten in Buenos Aires, 2006. / Descendants of the Ostermanns get together with German relatives in Buenos Aires, 2006.

Sammlung Deutsches Auswandererhaus / Collection German Emigration Center

haupt nicht. Auf Umwegen, mit etwas Glück und einem Stück Land des englischen Unternehmens Liebig landete die Truppe letztendlich in der argentinischen Provinz Corrientes, wo sie ihr Projekt verwirklichen konnte. Durch viel Mut und harte Arbeit entwickelte sich an dem Ort die bis heute bestehende „Colonia Liebig". Die Produktion von Mate-Tee, dem argentinischen Nationalgetränk, wurde zum Wirtschaftsfaktor Nummer Eins der Kolonie. Der Kontakt nach Deutschland brach nie ab und wird von den Nachkommen bei großen Familientreffen gepflegt.

In den Jahren nach der Machterteilung an die Nationalsozialisten im Jahr 1933 hofften viele deutsch-jüdische Familien auf ein Leben ohne Verfolgung in Argentinien. Wenn auch mit zunehmenden Einschränkungen und nicht immer auf dem direkten Weg fanden Flüchtlinge am Río de la Plata eine sichere Bleibe.

Die Familie von **Hermann Ehrenhaus** hält trotz des schweren Schicksals bis heute Verbindungen nach Deutschland. 14-jährig erfuhr Hermann, dass ihn die „Nürnberger Gesetze" von 1935 zum „Halbjuden" erklärten. Hermanns Vater war ein unter dem Künstlernamen Otto Ehrhardt weltbekannt gewordener Opernregisseur und guter Freund von Richard Strauss. Das Arbeitsverbot für jüdische Musiker in Deutschland zwang ihn zunächst nach Wien, später nach Bern. Weiter, immer weiter. Aber wohin? Wo hätte er Arbeit finden können?

In der Übersiedlung nach Argentinien sah der Vater die letzte Chance, seine Familie finanziell über Wasser halten zu können. Das „Teatro Colón" in Buenos Aires engagierte ihn; er nahm seine Familie mit. So bekam auch Hermann die Chance, einen Neuanfang zu wagen. Neu war für ihn vor allem die Sprache, die ihn daran hinderte, seine Schullauf-

...hofften viele deutsch-jüdische Familien auf ein Leben ohne Verfolgung in Argentinien.
...many German-Jewish families hoped to find a life without persecution in Argentina.

Over the course of the years, ties with Germany never broke off. Descendants of the immigrants continued to stay in touch and cultivate their relationship with Germany by means of large family get-togethers.

Familie Ehrenhaus / Ehrenhaus Family

Hermann Ehrenhaus

***04.03.1921 Düsseldorf (heute / today: Nordrhein-Westfalen);**
† 08.03.2006 Buenos Aires, Argentinien / Argentina

Die erste Zeit in Buenos Aires: Margaretha Fritz, Klaus, Hermann und Martin, 1940/1941. / Beginning in Buenos Aires: Margaretha Fritz, Klaus, Hermann and Martin, 1940/1941.

In the years after the National Socialists' accession to power in 1933, many German-Jewish families hoped to find a life without persecution in Argentina. Despite increasing restrictions and frequently circuitous routes a great number of refugees and emigrants did eventually find a safe place to live along the Río de la Plata. Bidding farewell to home and family was one of the hardest things emigrants had to do. Silence was one means of coping when memories became too painful to bear; some even attempted to cap the bond of past memories. Not so with the family of **Hermann Ehrenhaus**, who despite severe blows of fate continued to stay in close touch with Germany. As a 14-year old, Hermann found out that according to the Nuremberg Laws of 1935 he was a "half-Jew." Hermann's father, who had

bahn fortzuführen. Alternativ besuchte er das Konservatorium und wurde in kurzer Zeit zu einem hervorragenden Oboisten. Die Musikerkarriere ließ die Gedanken an eine Rückkehr der Familien nach Deutschland mit der Zeit verblassen – nicht aber die Erinnerungen an die alte Heimat. Die Verbundenheit wurde an die nächste Generation weitergegeben. Besonders die Sprache verband die Generationen. „Mit meinen Großeltern habe ich immer deutsch gesprochen. Es war die Familiensprache", sagt die Tochter Betina Ruth Ehrenhaus heute rückblickend. Während der letzten Militärdiktatur (1976–1983) wurde Tochter Betina zusammen mit ihrem Lebenspartner entführt und verschleppt. Der deutsche Pass, den Betina Ehrenhaus bei sich trug, rettete ihr wahrscheinlich das Leben. Sie kam frei. Ihren Mann sah sie jedoch nie wieder. Heute engagiert sich die Menschenrechtlerin für deutschstämmige Familien, die während der Diktatur Angehörige verloren haben.

Hermann Ehrenhaus (1. Oboe, li.) im „Orquesta Filarmónica de Buenos Aires", um 1970. / Hermann Ehrenhaus (1st oboe, le.) in the *Orquesta Filarmónica de Buenos Aires*, about 1970.

Familie Ehrenhaus / Ehrenhaus Family

attained world renown as an opera director and went by the professional name Otto Ehrhardt, was also a good friend of Richard Strauss. With the purge of Jewish artists and the Nazi-enforced work prohibition for Jews, Ehrhardt was forced to move first to Vienna (Austria), then to Bern (Switzerland). Farther, always farther. But where? Where could he find work?

> **Während der letzten Militärdiktatur (1976–1983) wurde Tochter Betina zusammen mit ihrem Lebenspartner entführt und verschleppt. / Under the last military dictatorship (1976–1983) Betina and her partner were kidnapped and abducted.**

Hermann's father saw Argentina as his last chance to maintain the family financially. The *Teatro Colón* in Buenos Aires hired Otto Ehrhardt, bringing his family over as well, a chance for Hermann to start a new life. The new language prevented him from continuing his school education. Instead, he attended the Conservatory and it wasn't long before he had become an outstanding oboist. Any thoughts the family had entertained of returning to Germany gradually faded as his musical career took off. However, memories of their former homeland—*Heimat*—never paled.

This feeling of attachment was passed on to the next generation. Language particularly was the bonding element between generations. In retrospect, daughter Betina Ruth Ehrenhaus today explains, "I always spoke German with my grandparents. It was the language of our family." Under the last military dictatorship (1976–1983) Betina and her partner were kidnapped and abducted. While Betina was released, saved probably by the German passport she was carrying at the time, her long-time partner disappeared, never to be seen again. Today, Betina Ehrenhaus works as a human-rights activist and is dedicated to helping families of German origin who lost members of their families during the dictatorship.

DIE ARCHITEKTUR / THE ARCHITECTURE

79

DIE ARCHITEKTUR

THE ARCHITECTURE

Skizze: / Sketch: Andreas Heller

ANDREAS HELLER

Ein Gemälde aus dem späten 19. Jahrhundert * steht am Anfang der Gestaltung für die Architektur des Deutschen Auswandererhauses: Eine Menschenmenge steht an der Kaje, verabschiedet ein Schiff mit vielen Menschen an Bord, die Europa in Richtung Amerika für immer verlassen. Eine Frau sticht aus dieser Menge heraus. Sie schwenkt ein weißes Tuch, winkt zum Abschied: für die Entwicklung der Formensprache der Architektur ein bleibender und prägender Eindruck. Diese Geste, die sich aus der Menge erhebt, ist Sinnbild für die Hoffnung, sich eines Tages wiederzusehen.

In the beginning of the conceptual design for the architecture of the German Emigration Center there was a nineteenth-century painting * depicting a crowd on the wharf bidding a shipful of passengers farewell as the ship casts off, heading for America. One woman stands out. She is waving a white hanky, waving farewell. This one little detail left a lasting and indelible impression, consequently influencing the development of the museum's architectural concept considerably. This small gesture, standing out from the crowd, was a symbol of hope; the hope that one day the passenger on board the ship leaving Europe for the New World and the person standing in the crowd of onlookers on the wharf and waving that passenger off would see each other again.

* → Siehe Glossar S. 111. / → See Glossary p. 111.

W. Huthmacher

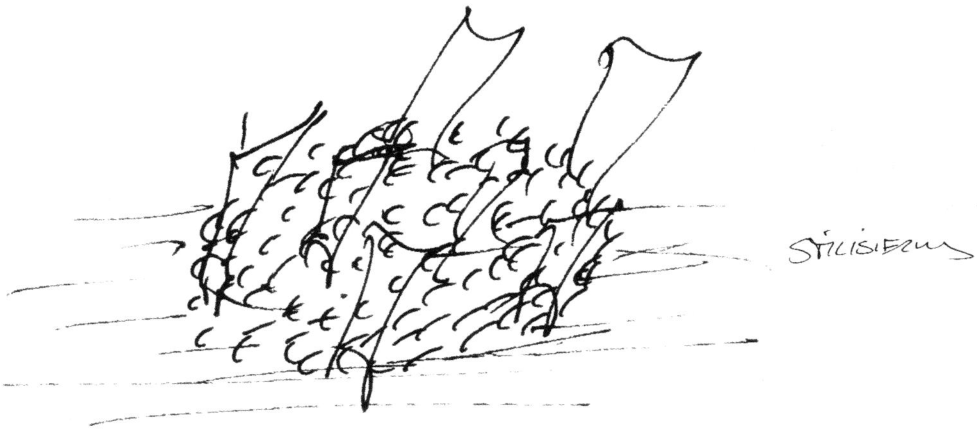

Skizze: / Sketch: Andreas Heller

Die aufragenden Schwingen des Gebäudes symbolisieren dieses winkende Tuch: hoch geschwungen und für ihre Größe zart. Eingebettet sind die Schwingen, manchmal auch Segel genannt, in eine runde, weiche Gebäudeform. Alles aus Sichtbeton.

The soaring wings of the structure symbolize that white handkerchief being waved in the air. Embedded in the round, soft shape of the building these wings, also called sails, rise high above the building, yet they are delicate for their size. The basic structure and the wings are made of exposed concrete.

W. Huthmacher

Eingeschnitten in diese Form: Ein kantiges, mit Holzlamellen beplanktes Obergeschoss, das sich ganz deutlich in die amorphe Form hineinschiebt. Ein Oxymoron, das die beiden Seiten der Lebenswege der Auswanderer beschreibt: Sehnsucht und Hoffnung auf der einen, harte Schicksalsschläge auf der anderen.

The second floor, angular in shape and set into the amorphous structure, is covered with wooden slats, creating an oxymoron characterizing both sides of the emigrants' lives—on the one hand, hope and longing, on the other, hardship and strokes of fate.

Auf über 4.500 Quadratmetern ist dieses Gebäude Heimat für zigtausende Biographien. Sie stehen stellvertretend für Menschen, die sich in ihrem Leben auf den Weg machen. Wir haben mit Bedacht keine historisierende Formensprache gewählt, um zu zeigen, dass auch Migration heute und morgen ein Thema für das Deutsche Auswandererhaus ist.

In a space comprising 4,500 square meters, this structure is home to umpteen biographies, representing all those who set out on an unknown path during their lifetimes. We deliberately chose modern architecture for this museum, because migration is a constant and hence always a current topic.

W. Huthmacher

W. Huthmacher

SONDERAUSSTELLUNGEN / SPECIAL EXHIBITIONS

Orte + Biographien
Die Sonderausstellungsthemen 2006–2009

Sites + Biographies
Special Exhibition Themes 2006–2009

SIMONE EICK, KATRIN QUIRIN

„Alles fließt." Heraklits Aphorismus ist das Credo des homo migrans, des wandernden Menschen. Trotzdem – in diesem stetig wogenden, anonymen Menschenmeer, das schon immer von Dorf zu Dorf, von Land zu Land, von Kontinent zu Kontinent zog – gibt es herausragende Landmarken und Menschen.

Die Zielorte steigen in den Träumen der Auswanderungswilligen zu Sehnsuchtsorten auf; später, wenn man angekommen ist, bietet die neue Lebenswelt Chancen auf den gesellschaftlichen Aufstieg. Dort werden sie heiraten, Kinder bekommen, begraben sein. Im schlimmsten Fall ist die neue Heimat ein Ort des Scheiterns.

Die Biographien sind im Deutschen Auswandererhaus beispielhafte Lebensgeschichten von einfachen Menschen und von Menschen, die Herausragendes geleistet haben.

In seinen Sonderausstellungen widmet sich das Deutsche Auswandererhaus Orten und Biographien, um das Phänomen Auswanderung noch eindringlicher vorstellen zu können.

"Everything flows." This famous aphorism attributed to Heraclitus is the creed of the homo migrans, i.e. migrant man. Nevertheless, in this anonymous and continuously flowing sea of mankind—from village to village, country to country, continent to continent—there are landmarks and individuals which stand out.

In the minds and hearts of those wishing to emigrate, the destination of choice becomes the place they long to be. Later, on reaching that destination, the new environment offers the chance of social advancement. Here is where they will marry and have children, and eventually be buried. At worst, the new home might spell failure for the immigrant.

The biographies at the German Emigration Center are exemplary stories of simple people as well as of people who achieved great things.

The German Emigration Center dedicates all special exhibitions to sites and biographies as a means of presenting the phenomenon of migration more vividly.

Orte/Sites

Pacific Palisades

Kalifornien, USA
California, U.S.A.

Feuchtwanger Memorial Library, University of Southern California Libraries, Special Collections

SCHRIFTSTELLER IM EXIL
WRITERS IN EXILE

Thomas Mann, Lion Feuchtwanger, Vicki Baum, Bertolt Brecht und Theodor W. Adorno gehörten zu der Gruppe von Schriftstellern, die sich während der nationalsozialistischen Diktatur im Ort Pacific Palisades in Kalifornien im Exil niederließen. Lebens- und Arbeitsbedingungen in der englischsprachigen Fremde stellten für alle deutschsprachigen Schriftsteller eine Herausforderung dar. Pacific Palisades – eine Hügellandschaft im Norden von Los Angeles – wurde zum „Weimar unter Palmen". Doch das Paradies hatte seine Schattenseiten: Nicht allen Schriftstellern gelang es, in Amerika Fuß zu fassen. / Thomas Mann, Lion Feuchtwanger, Vicki Baum, Bertolt Brecht and Theodor W. Adorno numbered among the writers who fled Germany and its Nazi dictatorship to live in exile in Pacific Palisades. The living and working conditions in an English-language environment far away from home posed a challenge for these German-language writers. Pacific Palisades, in the hills north of Los Angeles, soon became a "tropical Weimar" of sorts. What at first glance may have appeared to be paradise definitely had its drawbacks. Not all of the émigré writers managed to cope with their new lives in the U.S.A.

28.01.–02.04.2006

Pacific Palisades – Der Weg deutschsprachiger Schriftsteller ins kalifornische Exil 1932–1941 / Pacific Palisades – German-Language Writers on the Road to Exile in California 1932–1941

In Kooperation mit dem Buddenbrookhaus Lübeck. Außerdem gezeigt im Literaturhaus München, Buddenbrookhaus Lübeck und Erich Maria Remarque-Friedenszentrum Osnabrück. / In cooperation with the Buddenbrookhaus Lübeck. Also shown at Literaturhaus Munich, Buddenbrookhaus Lübeck and Erich Maria Remarque-Friedenszentrum Osnabrück.

Zu dieser Sonderausstellung ist ein Katalog in der edition DAH erschienen. / A catalogue of this special exhibition was published by edition DAH.

DAH

DAH

Sammlung / Collection Arnold Kludas

DAH

Buenos Aires

Hauptstadt Argentiniens / Capital of Argentina

EINE STADT VOLLER HISTORISCHER GEGENSÄTZE
A CITY FULL OF HISTORIC CONTRASTS

Die deutschen Einwanderer in Argentinien waren lange Zeit sehr präsent in der Öffentlichkeit: Zeitungen, Gebäude, Firmen und Siedlungen mit deutschen Namen gab es zahlreiche. Sie alle wiesen hin auf die knapp 100.000 Deutschen, die ins Land gekommen waren, um dort als Bauern, Arbeiter und Handwerker ein neues Leben zu beginnen. Mit Beginn der nationalsozialistischen Diktatur traten zwei andere Einwanderergruppen in den Vordergrund: jüdische Flüchtlinge, später dann NS-Verbrecher. So begegneten sich in der Stadt Opfer, Täter und argentinische Sympathisanten des Nationalsozialismus. Die Geschichte fand eine tragische Fortsetzung: Nachkommen der jüdischen Flüchtlinge wurden zu Opfern der argentinischen Militärdiktatur in den 1970er Jahren. Exklusiv für das Museumskino entstand der Kurzfilm „24h Buenos Aires" vom Grimme-Preisträger Ciro Cappellari. Drei argentinische Biographien sind auch in der Dauerausstellung vertreten. / German immigrants to Argentina were very present in public life in Argentina for a long time. Newspapers, buildings, businesses and settlements with German names were numerous, all indicative of the nearly 100,000 Germans who came to the country to start a new life as farmers, blue-collar workers and workmen. With the beginning of the Nazi dictatorship two new emigrant groups came to the fore—Jewish refugees and, later, Nazi criminals. Buenos Aires became a place where victims, perpetrators and sympathizers of the Nazi dictatorship encountered one another. History repeated itself tragically when descendants of the Jewish refugees became victims of the military dictatorship in Argentina in the 1970s. The short film *24h Buenos Aires* was created by Grimme award-winning director Ciro Cappellari exclusively for the museum's Ocean Cinema. The permanent exhibition features three Argentinean biographies.

21.01.–21.09.2008

Nach Buenos Aires! Deutsche Auswanderer und Flüchtlinge im 20. Jahrhundert / Off to Buenos Aires! German Emigrants and Refugees in the 20th Century

Zu dieser Sonderausstellung ist ein Katalog in der edition DAH erschienen. / A catalogue of this special exhibition was published by edition DAH.

C. Cappellari

C. Cappellari

C. Cappellari

C. Cappellari

Handelskammer Bremen / Bremen Chamber of Commerce

DAH

DAH

New Orleans
Louisiana, U.S.A.

K. Quirin

DAH

DIE AUSGEWANDERTE STADT
THE CITY LEFT BEHIND

Der Wirbelsturm „Katrina" erreichte am 29. August 2005 New Orleans. 1.836 Menschen starben und 1,3 Millionen flohen aus der Stadt und ihrer Umgebung. New Orleans fehlen bis heute 40 Prozent seiner ehemaligen Bewohner. Die meisten leben nun im ländlichen Louisiana und Texas. Binnenmigration aufgrund von Klimakatastrophen ist ein neues Migrationsphänomen, das die nächsten Jahrzehnte bestimmen wird. / Hurricane *Katrina* hit New Orleans on 29 August 2005 killing 1,836 people and forcing 1.3 million to flee the city and its surroundings. Today, New Orleans is still missing forty percent of its former population. The majority has taken up residence elsewhere in the state of Louisiana or relocated to Texas. Domestic migration due to climate disaster is a migration phenomenon destined to mark the coming decades.

02.02.–10.05.2009

Nach der Flut die Flucht. New Orleans – die ausgewanderte Stadt / The Flight after the Flood. New Orleans—The City Left Behind

Zur Sonderausstellung wurden Kurzfilmbiographien gedreht. / Short biographical films were produced for the special exhibition.

J. Meier

„Die Sintflut, seit Anbeginn Schreckensvision der Menschen, schien angebrochen.“
Der Spiegel, 1962
„(...) und da versank während eines schlimmen Tages und einer schlimmen Nacht das ganze streitbare Geschlecht bei euch scharenweise unter die Erde, und ebenso verschwand die Insel Atlantis, indem sie im Meere unterging.“
Platon, 360 v.d.Z.
Kelcy & Jim Patterson
Richard Kuntz
David Winger
The Jackson Family
They Never Came Back
Aufbauprojekte – Eine Stadt verändert sich / Restoration Projects – The City is Changing
Rückkehr unmöglich? / Die Neue Heimat / Impossible to Return? / A New Home

Biographien/Biographies

Augustus Sherman

EIN EINWANDERUNGSINSPEKTOR UND SEINE PORTRAITS
AN IMMIGRATION INSPECTOR AND HIS PORTRAITS

Fasziniert von der Vielzahl der Nationen nutzte der Einwanderungsbeamte Augustus F. Sherman sein geschultes Auge, um mit seiner Fotokamera die mannigfaltigen Eindrücke auf Ellis Island festzuhalten. Zwischen 1905 und 1925 fertigte er etwa 250 Fotografien von Immigranten – Serielle Aufnahmen, die sich in Aufbau und Motiv ähneln. Die Fotografie dient dabei als eine vermeintlich unbestechliche, objektive Technik, die die stereotype Vorstellung von Einwanderern illustriert. Fascinated by the diversity of cultures and ethnic peoples immigration officer Augustus F. Sherman used his trained eye to photograph the variety of impressions of Ellis Island. Between 1905 and 1925, he took about 250 photographs of immigrants—serial portraits resembling one another in composition and motif. Photography is a supposedly unerring, objective technique illustrating the stereotype image of immigrants.

10.03.–14.05.2006

Augustus F. Sherman: Ellis Island Portraits 1905–1920. *Fotoausstellung im Deutschen Auswandererhaus in Kooperation mit dem Ellis Island Immigration Museum. /* ***Augustus F. Sherman: Ellis Island Portraits 1905–1920.*** *Photo exhibition at the German Emigration Center in cooperation with the Ellis Island Immigration Museum.*

Felix Schlesinger

GESCHICHTE EINES BILDES / THE STORY OF A PICTURE

Der Künstler Felix Schlesinger wusste wie man Geld verdiente – auch in den USA: Harmonische Familienidyllen aus Deutschland und idealisierte Rheinlandschaften stellten für die deutschen Einwanderer in den USA äußerst beliebte Motive dar. Sein Gemälde „In der Pass- und Polizeistube vor der Emigration" von 1859 fällt etwas aus Rahmen. Es greift eine tagesaktuelle Situation auf. Gezeigt wird der Moment, der existentiell für die Auswanderer war: die Ausstellung des Passes in einer Amtsstube. Ohne Pass konnte man in dieser Zeit der deutschen Vielstaaterei noch nicht einmal den Auswanderungshafen erreichen.

Zweifelhaft, ob Schlesinger mit diesem Motiv, das er in drei Variationen malte, viel Geld verdiente, aber er schuf ein einzigartiges sozialhistorisches Dokument. Je ein Gemälde hängt heute im Deutschen Auswandererhaus, im Deutschen Historischen Museum Berlin und im hamburgmuseum. / Artist Felix Schlesinger knew how to make money, also in the U.S.A. Family scenes full of idyllic harmony and idealized scenes along the Rhine River were favorites among German immigrants to the United States. His painting entitled *The Passport and Police Dispatch Prior to Emigration* from 1859 is rather unusual. It depicts a most typical scene of the time, an existentially important moment for any emigrant, the issuing of a passport at the police dispatch. At the time Germany was a hodgepodge of small states; without a passport it was next to impossible to even travel to the German port of emigration.

It is arguable whether this painting, which Schlesinger executed in three variations, sold well, but it certainly created a unique sociohistorical document. Today, one each of the three paintings hangs in the German Emigration Center, the Deutsches Historisches Museum Berlin and the hamburgmuseum.

02.10.2006–28.01.2007

Felix Schlesingers „In der Pass- und Polizeistube vor der Emigration" (1859). Geschichte eines Bildes */ Felix Schlesinger's "The Passport and Police Dispatch Prior to Emigration" (1859)—The Story of a Picture.*

DAH

Hoffnungsträger
Bearer of Hope

„HOFFNUNG – DIE ZWEITE SEELE DER UNGLÜCKLICHEN?"* / "HOPE—THE SECOND SOUL OF THE UNHAPPY?"*

Europas ausgewanderte 1848er Revolutionäre, Arbeiterführer, Frauenrechtlerinnen, Zionisten und Shoa-Überlebende einte eines: Die Hoffnung, dass in einer neuen Heimat etwas besser werden würde. Ihre kulturellen Wurzeln, die abrahamitischen Religionen Judentum, Christentum und Islam, predigen die Hoffnung. Der stärkste atheistische Hoffnungsmythos ist derjenige der Pandora. Die Annäherung an die treibende Kraft der Auswanderer, die Hoffnung, steht ganz im Zeichen der Zeit und mus s immer wieder neu erfolgen. (* J.W. von Goethe in „Maxime und Reflexionen", 1833.) / One thing united European émigrés—revolutionaries from 1848, labor leaders, women's suffragettes, Zionists and Shoa survivors—the hope of having a better life in a new country. Their cultural roots, the Abrahamic religions Judaism, Christianity and Islam, are based on hope. The strongest atheist myth of hope is Pandora's Box. The emigrant's driving force—hope—is quite a sign of the times and must be approached over and over again. (* J.W. von Goethe in *Maxime und Reflexionen,* 1833.)

28.02.–30.04.2007

Hoffnung – Die zweite Seele der Unglücklichen?
Hope—The Second Soul of the Unhappy?

Carl Stangen

PAUSCHALREISENDE AUF AUSWANDERERSCHIFFEN
THE FIRST ORGANIZED TRIP ON EMIGRANT SHIPS

Amerika wurde im 19. Jahrhundert das „Gelobte Land" genannt. Gut situierte Europäer wollten trotzdem nicht ins Land der unbegrenzten Möglichkeiten auswandern, aber sie wollten es kennenlernen. Der Reiseveranstalter Stangen führte 1893 anlässlich der Weltausstellung in Chicago eine Pauschalreise durch. Ein voller Erfolg: Ausgebucht unternahm die Reisegesellschaft die 84tägige Fahrt von Bremerhaven mit dem Dampfschiff „Saale" nach New York und reiste von dort mit der Eisenbahn von New York, Washington und Chicago zu den Naturwundern im Westen der USA. / In the 19th century, America became the "promised land." While affluent Europeans did not wantto emigrate to the land of unlimited opportunity, they did want to see it. A travel operator by the name of Stangen organized a package trip to the United States in 1893, the year of the World's Fair in Chicago. And a success it was. A fully booked tour group embarked on an 84-day journey departing from Bremerhaven on board the steamship *Saale* for New York from where the group toured the cities of New York, Washington, D.C. and Chicago, as well as the natural wonders of the West, by railway.

06.05.–29.07.2007

Stangen's Party – Die erste deutsche Pauschalreise in die Neue Welt. *Fotoausstellung in Kooperation mit dem Leibniz-Institut für Länderkunde e.V. /* ***Stangen's Party—The First Organized Trip to the U.S.A.*** *Photo exhibition in joint cooperation with the Leibniz Institute for Regional Geography.*

Leibniz-Institut für Länderkunde · Leipzig

S. Volk

S. Volk

Lena

PORTRAIT EINER SPÄTAUSSIEDLERIN
PORTRAIT OF A LATE REPATRIATE

Lena lebt heute in Paderborn und arbeitet als Erzieherin in einem Kindergarten. 2004 verließ sie ihre sibirische Heimatstadt Slawgorod und kam über das Grenzdurchgangslager Friedland nach Deutschland. Der Fotograf Stefan Volk begleitete Lena auf ihrem Weg in die neue Heimat über fünf Jahre. Ein einzigartiges Portrait, das beispielhaft für den Weg der rund 4,4 Millionen Aussiedler und Spätaussiedler steht.
Stefan Volk wurde 1971 in Münster geboren. Nach einer Fotografenlehre studierte er Fotodesign an der FH Bielefeld. Stefan Volk lebt in Hamburg und arbeitet in den Bereichen Reportage, Reise und Portrait, u. a. für „GEO", „Stern" und „Brigitte". / Lena lives in Paderborn today where she works as a kindergarten teacher. In 2004 she left her hometown Slavgorod in Siberia, entering Germany through the Border Repatriation Center in Friedland. Photographer Stefan Volk accompanied Lena for five years on her path to a new homeland. A unique portrait, exemplary of the path of some 4.4 million ethnic Germans and late repatriates of German origin.
Stefan Volk was born in Münster in 1971. After apprenticing with a photographer he studied Photographic Design at the Bielefeld University of Applied Sciences. Stefan Volk lives in Hamburg and carries out reportage, travel and portrait assignments for magazines such as *GEO*, *Stern* and *Brigitte*.

23.11.2008–15.01.2009
25.05.–31.12.2009

Lena. Portrait einer deutsch-russischen Auswanderung 2003–2008 / Lena. Portrait of a German-Russian Emigrant 2003–2008

Zu dieser Sonderausstellung ist ein Katalog in der edition DAH erschienen. / A catalogue of this special exhibition was published by edition DAH.

S. Volk

S. Volk

GLOSSAR / GLOSSARY

GLOSSAR

A

Abschied > Ein „Lebe wohl!" für immer oder auf Zeit.

AEMI – The Association of European Migration Institutions > Das Kooperationsforum europäischer Institutionen und Organisationen, die sich mit historischer und aktueller Migration befassen, organisiert internationale Symposien und gemeinschaftliche Forschungsprojekte.
> www.aemi.dk

Akkulturation / Assimilation > Akkulturation ist ein Begriff aus der Migrationsforschung, der Integrationsprozesse in Einwanderergesellschaften beschreibt. Ethnologen, Soziologen und Historiker bezeichnen damit die Angleichung verschiedener Kulturen innerhalb einer Gesellschaft. Diesen Prozess des kulturellen Austauschs durchleben sowohl die Immigranten als auch die einheimischen Bürger des Aufnahmelandes. Er kann mehrere Generationen und damit Jahrzehnte dauern. Ein erster Austausch zeigt sich beispielsweise in der Übernahme und/oder dem Tolerieren von Essgewohnheiten oder religiösen und politischen Feiertagen. Jeder Einwanderer verfolgt dabei eine eigene Strategie: Während einige die Integration, also die Eingliederung in die Aufnahmegesellschaft wünschen, separieren und isolieren sich andere. Der Idealfall ist eine Integration unter Beibehaltung eigener kultureller Wurzeln. Über Erfolg oder Misserfolg der Integration entscheiden Gesellschaft und Politik des Aufnahmelandes.
Der Begriff der Assimilation gilt in der heutigen Migrationsforschung als veraltet. Er bezeichnet die Aufgabe der ursprünglichen kulturellen Identität von Einwanderern. Die Vorstellung, dass die Einwanderer beim Grenzübertritt ihr kulturelles Gepäck abgeben, hat sich bei der Untersuchung verschiedener Einwanderergesellschaften wie den USA, aber auch Deutschland als falsch erwiesen. Siehe auch → **Melting Pot / Salad Bowl**

Arbeitsmigranten > Sie planen eine Auswanderung auf Zeit, um in einem anderen Land zu arbeiten. Schon immer waren wirtschaftliche Motive Hauptgrund für eine Auswanderung.
Während des so genannten Wirtschaftswunders der 1950er Jahre herrschte in der Bundesrepublik Deutschland ein Mangel an Arbeitskräften. Vom Ende der 1950er Jahre bis zum Anwerbestopp 1973 kamen rund 14 Millionen Arbeitsmigranten vor allem aus der Türkei, Italien und Spanien ins Land. Elf Millionen kehrten in ihr Heimatland zurück, die anderen blieben, holten ihre Familien nach und siedelten dauerhaft in der BRD an. Auch in der DDR wurden in geringem Umfang ausländische Arbeitskräfte beschäftigt, vor allem aus Vietnam.

Asyl > Schon seit Jahrhunderten bieten Freistädte, Hospize oder Klöster schutzbedürftigen und verfolgten Menschen Unterschlupf. Heute versteht man unter Asyl vor allem die Anerkennung politischer Flüchtlinge. In Artikel 16 des Grundgesetzes der Bundesrepublik Deutschland ist das Grundrecht auf Asyl für politisch Verfolgte festgeschrieben. Dieses weltweit offenste Asylrecht wurde 1993 jedoch stark eingeschränkt. Seitdem hat kaum noch eine Chance auf Asyl, wer aus „verfolgungsfreien" Ländern stammt oder über „sichere Drittstaaten" in die Bundesrepublik eingereist ist. Während ihres Verfahrens, das zwischen zwei Wochen und mehreren Jahren dauern kann, müssen Asylsuchende in ihnen zugewiesenen Unterkünften wohnen und dürfen ihren Aufenthaltsort nicht ohne Genehmigung verlassen. Sie erhalten geringere Sozialleistungen als üblich und in manchen Bundesländern statt Geld Lebensmittelgutscheine oder -pakete. Seit 2001 dürfen Asylbewerber und geduldete Ausländer nach einem Jahr Wartezeit arbeiten, wenn sich für die Stelle kein deutscher Arbeitnehmer oder ein Ausländer mit Aufenthaltsbewilligung findet. Asylberechtigte bekommen zunächst eine Aufenthaltserlaubnis für drei Jahre, danach, wenn kein Widerruf erfolgt, eine Niederlassungserlaubnis.

Aussiedler / Spätaussiedler > Aussiedler sind Angehörige deutschstämmiger Minderheiten, deren Vorfahren sich seit dem Mittelalter bis in das 19. Jahrhundert auf den Gebieten nahezu aller Staaten Ost- und Südosteuropas angesiedelt hatten – dem Ruf nach Arbeitskräften und Siedlern vor allem der russischen Zaren folgend.
Seit 1950 hat die Bundesrepublik Deutschland über vier Millionen Aussiedler vor allem aus der Sowjetunion bzw. der GUS aufgenommen. Das „Bundesvertriebenen- und Flüchtlingsgesetz" von 1953 sicherte ihnen die deutsche Staatsangehörigkeit und integrationsfördernde Maßnahmen zu. Seit 1993 werden Aussiedler aus anderen Staaten als der GUS nur anerkannt, wenn sie eine Benachteiligung aufgrund ihrer deutschen Volkszugehörigkeit nachweisen können. Antragsberechtigt sind seither außerdem nur noch vor 1993 geborene Spätaussiedler. Als zusätzliche Barriere wurde 1996 ein Sprachtest eingeführt, der seit 2005 auch für mitreisende Familienangehörige nichtdeutscher Herkunft verpflichtend ist.

Auswanderer > Menschen, die die Absicht haben, sich für immer in einem fremden Land niederzulassen.

Auswandereragenten > Für Reedereien und Schiffsmakler übernahmen Auswandereragenten überall in Europa die Anwerbung von Ausreisewilligen.

Auswandererhaus > Als bis dahin weltweit einmalige Einrichtung 1849 von dem Bremer Kaufmann Johann Georg Claussen in Bremerhaven eröffnet, bot das Auswandererhaus, auch „Karlsburg" genannt, bis zu 2.000 Reisenden Kost und Logis zu erheblich günstigeren Preisen und in besseren hygienischen Verhältnissen als in den hafennahen Wirtschaften und Spelunken.

Auswanderungshäfen > Die bedeutendsten Einschiffungshäfen für deutsche Auswanderer waren bis in die Mitte des 19. Jahrhunderts Rotterdam (Holland), Antwerpen (Belgien), Le Havre (Frankreich) sowie Liverpool und Southampton (England). Auswanderer aus Süd- und Südosteuropa reisten zumeist von Genua (Italien) ab. Dank der → **Bremer Verordnung,** der Einrichtung eines → **Auswandererhauses** und der weltweit erfolgreichen Reederei → **Norddeutscher Lloyd**

Staatsarchiv Bremen

Bei der Mahlzeit: Auswanderer im Speisesaal der Bremer „Missler-Hallen", um 1910. / Mealtime: Emigrants eating in the *Missler Halls* in Bremen, about 1910.

Historisches Archiv der Hapag-Lloyd AG

Der Hamburger Reeder Albert Ballin. / The Hamburg shipowner Albert Ballin.

begann Mitte des 19. Jahrhunderts Bremerhavens Aufstieg zum größten deutschen Auswandererhafen. Der „Norddeutsche Lloyd" hatte seinen Heimathafen in Bremerhaven, seine Schiffe fuhren jedoch unter Bremer Flagge, da Bremerhaven zum Staat Bremen gehörte und immer noch gehört. Insgesamt wanderten zwischen 1830 und 1974 7,2 Millionen Menschen von Bremerhaven in die Neue Welt aus.
Während in der Segelschiffzeit und in der frühen Dampfschiffszeit auch von Hamburg Auswandererschiffe in die Neue Welt aufbrachen, änderte sich dies Ende des 19. Jahrhunderts: In Hamburg lag der Sitz der Passagierdampfschifffahrtsgesellschaft → **Hapag**, deren Schiffe ab 1889 größtenteils vom verkehrstechnisch günstiger gelegenen Cuxhaven abfuhren. Insgesamt reisten auf Schiffen unter der Hamburger Flagge 5,5 Millionen Passagiere in die Neue Welt.
Das südfranzösische Marseille erlangte vor allem während der Zeit des Nationalsozialismus als Flüchtlingshafen Bedeutung.

Auswanderungswellen > Wanderungsstatistiken werden oft als Liniendiagramme dargestellt. Die Aufwärtsbewegungen im Wanderungsgeschehen werden dabei als Wellen bezeichnet. Sucht man nach Gründen für solche Höhepunkte der Auswanderungen, zeigt es sich oft, dass die Menschen mit einer Verzögerung von fünf bis zehn Jahren auf Wirtschaftskrisen reagieren. Im 19. Jahrhundert kamen Missernten und die darauf folgenden Hungersnöte als weitere Auswanderungsgründe hinzu. Am verheerendsten trafen die Ernteausfälle Irland: Ausgelöst durch aufeinander folgende Kartoffel-Missernten zwischen 1846 und 1851 verhungerten etwa eine Million Menschen, eine weitere Million Iren verließen das Land. Siehe auch → **Kettenwanderung**

B

Ballin, Albert > Der jüngste Sohn eines jüdischen Kaufmanns (1857–1918) begann seine Karriere bei der → **Hapag** im Jahre 1886. Schnell übertrug die Hamburger Reederei ihrem Angestellten leitende Aufgaben. Bereits 1888 war er Direktor, 1899 Generaldirektor der Hapag. Ballin trug einen wesentlichen Anteil zum Aufstieg Hamburgs als Auswandererhafen bei. Siehe auch → **Veddel**

Bandoneon (-ion) > Das Bandoneon gehört zur Gruppe der Handbalginstrumente. In den 1870er Jahren gelangte es von Deutschland nach Argentinien. Dort entwickelte sich das Instrument schnell zum festen Bestandteil des Tangos.

Belgranodeutsch > Ein Sprachgemisch aus Deutsch und Spanisch, das noch heute von den deutschen Einwanderern und ihren Nachkommen gesprochen wird. Namensgeber ist der stark von Deutschen geprägte Stadtteil Belgrano in Buenos Aires.

Blaues Band > Die Verleihung des „Blauen Bandes" für die schnellste Atlantiküberquerung war im Zeitalter der Dampfschifffahrt für Reedereien eine bedeutende Ehrung. 1838 erhielt die „Sirius" als erstes Schiff diese Auszeichnung. Bis zur Jahrhundertwende dominierten die Schiffe englischer Gesellschaften das Feld, dann brach das Jahrzehnt der großen Schiffe des → **Norddeutschen Lloyd** und der → **Hapag** an. Als letzter großer Dampfer holte sich 1952 die „United States" das „Blaue Band".

Bremer Verordnung > Als erste staatliche Maßnahme zum Schutze der Auswanderer in Deutschland begründete die Bremer „Verordnung wegen der Auswanderer mit hiesigen oder fremden Schiffen" von 1832 Bremerhavens guten Ruf als Auswandererhafen entscheidend mit: Erstmals waren Reeder per Gesetz verpflichtet, die Seetüchtigkeit ihrer Schiffe nachzuweisen, Passagierlisten zu führen, ausreichend Proviant auch für

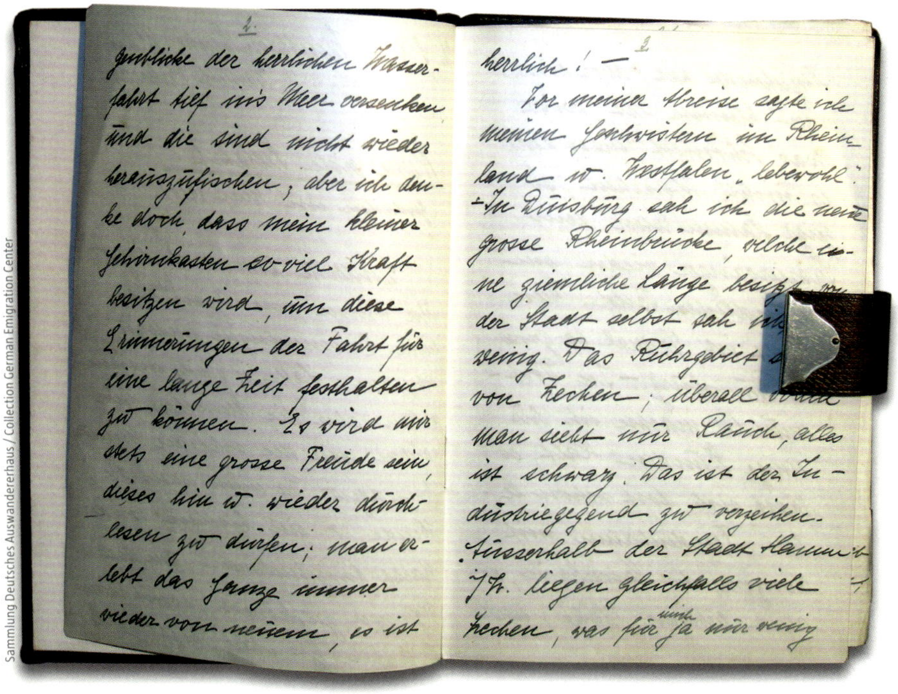

genblicke der herrlichen Wasser-
fahrt tief ins Meer versenken
und die sind nicht wieder
herauszufischen; aber ich den-
ke doch, dass mein kleiner
Gehirnkasten so-viel Kraft
besitzen wird, um diese
Erinnerungen der Fahrt für
eine lange Zeit festhalten
zu können. Es wird mir
stets eine grosse Freude sein,
dieses hin u. wieder durch-
lesen zu dürfen; man er-
lebt das Ganze immer
wieder von neuem, es ist

herrlich! —
Vor meiner Abreise sagte ich
meinen Geschwistern im Rhein-
land u. Westfalen „lebewohl".
In Duisburg sah ich die neue
grosse Rheinbrücke, welche ei-
ne ziemliche Länge besitzt, von
der Stadt selbst sah ich
wenig. Das Ruhrgebiet
von Zechen; überall
man sieht nur Rauch, alles
ist schwarz. Das ist der In-
dustriegegend zu verzeihen.
Ausserhalb der Stadt Hamm
i/W. liegen gleichfalls viele
Zechen, was für uns ja nur wenig

Sammlung Deutsches Auswandererhaus / Collection German Emigration Center

Reisebericht über eine Auswanderung nach Amerika, Verfasserin unbekannt, 1910. / An emigrant's journal of her journey to America, author unknown, 1910.

die Passagiere des Zwischendecks mitzuführen und weitere Mindeststandards auf den Schiffen einzuhalten.

C

Castle Garden > Castle Garden war Amerikas erste Einwanderungsstation. Sie lag für die Schiffe gut erreichbar an der Südspitze Manhattans. Der zentrale Ankunftsort bot den Einwanderern Schutz vor Wucherern und sie hatten dort die Möglichkeit, Eisenbahnfahrkarten für die Weiterfahrt ins Landesinnere zu erwerben. Hier wurden die Einwanderer auch in Ankunftslisten pro Schiff erfasst. Diese Ankunftslisten, im Englischen „Manifests" oder „Passenger Lists", dienen noch heute Familienforschern in aller Welt, um nach ihren Vorfahren zu suchen (siehe auch → **Datenbanken / Familienrecherche**). Von 1855 bis 1890 reisten über Castle Garden etwa acht Millionen Menschen nach Amerika ein. Abgelöst wurde Castle Garden von → **Ellis Island**.

Colonia Liebig > liegt im nördlichen Teil der Provinz Corrientes in Argentinien. Am 27. Januar 1924 wurde die Deutsch-Südamerikanische Kolonie und Handelsvereinigung (Cooperativa) „Neu Karlsruhe", wie das Dorf zuerst hieß, gegründet. Ursprünglich war das genossenschaftliche Siedlungsprojekt für Paraguay geplant worden. Die Pläne scheiterten und die ersten 200–300 deutschen Siedler erhielten in Corrientes Land der Liebig-Gesellschaft („Liebig Extract of Meat Company"), nach der der Ort benannt wurde. Im Dezember 1926 erfolgte dann die Gründung der „Cooperativa Agrícola de la Colonia Liebig", deren erster Präsident Walter Ostermann war. Bis heute produziert die Genossenschaft Mate-Tee.

Cunard Line > 1839 wurde die „Cunard Line" als „British and North American Royal Mail Steam Packet Company" (Umbenennung 1878) von dem Kanadier Samuel Cunard gegründet. Zunächst sollte sie eine zuverlässige Postzustellung zwischen Großbritannien und Nordamerika ermöglichen. Schon 1840 wurden die ersten vier Dampfschiffe in Betrieb genommen und ein wöchentlicher Service von Liverpool nach Halifax und Boston eingerichtet. Von Anfang an konnten auch regelmäßig Passagiere mitgenommen werden. Bis in die 1870er Jahre dominierte die „Cunard Line" das Post- und Passagiertransportwesen, litt aber unter den teils strengen Auflagen der Geldgeber.
1932 fusionierte die von der Weltwirtschaftskrise getroffene „Cunard Line" auf Druck der britischen Regierung mit der → **White Star Line** zur „Cunard White Star Line" und konzentrierte sich zunehmend auf das Geschäft mit Kreuzfahrten. 1998 schloss sie sich dem Kreuzfahrtenimperium der „Carnival Corporation" an.

Cuxhaven > Seit 1889 fertigte die Hamburger Reederei → **Hapag** ihre Schnelldampfer Richtung New York von der damals hamburgischen Stadt an der Elbemündung ab. Dafür ließ der Hamburger Staat die Hafenanlagen Cuxhavens ausbauen. 1902 wurde die Hapag-Halle als Überseebahnhof fertiggestellt. Als Dependance von Hamburg liegen bisher keine gesicherten Gesamtzahlen zur Auswanderung über Cuxhaven vor. Die meisten Schiffe steuerten Häfen in Nordamerika an. Nach dem Zweiten Weltkrieg nahm 1948 die „Cunard White Star Line" (→ **Cunard Line**) als erste Reederei ihren Liniendienst wieder auf. Von September 1948 bis März 1950 brachten ihre Schiffe „Samaria" und „Scythia" auf 27 Reisen 26.700 → **Displaced Persons** nach Kanada. 1968 kam in Cuxhaven durch die immer größere Konkurrenz durch den → **Luftverkehr** das Aus für die überseeischen Liniendienste.

D

Datenbanken / Familienrecherche > Verschiedene Datenbanken ermöglichen eine Recherche nach ausgewanderten Vorfahren im Internet:

Bremer Passagierlisten 1920–1939 (Die MAUS)
> www.passagierlisten.de
Im Archiv der Handelskammer Bremen lagern heute noch 2.953 Passagierlisten von Bremer Schiffe. Dies sind 70% der Passagierlisten von Schiffen, die zwischen 1920 und 1939 von Bremerhaven in die USA, nach Kanada, Südamerika und Australien gefahren sind. Seit Juli 1999 wurden diese Listen von der „Gesellschaft für Familienforschung Bremen e.V.", die MAUS, im Staatsarchiv Bremen erfasst. Alle weiteren Bremer Passagierlisten sind – bis auf wenige Ausnahmen – vernichtet worden. Die Listen nach 1945 stehen noch unter Datenschutz. Die Datenbank steht im Internet zur freien Verfügung.

Ancestry
> www.ancestry.com
Die US-amerikanische Firma Ancestry arbeitet mit dem Nationalarchiv in Washington zusammen: Im Archiv lagern die Passagierlisten der Schiffe, die aus aller Welt in US-amerikanische Häfen einliefen. Daneben sind auch die Hamburger Passagierlisten zu finden. Ebenfalls befinden sich dort die US-amerikanischen Listen der Volkszählungen, die seit 1790 alle zehn Jahre durchgeführt werden. Darüberhinaus bietet die Datenbank die Einsicht in ausgesuchte deutsche Auswandererregister, deutsche Telefon- und Adressbücher, sowie die Bremer Musterungslisten und Seeleuteregister.
Ancestry verarbeitet die Passagierlisten (bis 1957) und Volkszählungslisten elektronisch: Mit Scannern werden die Daten digitalisiert und im Internet zur Verfügung gestellt. Daneben gibt es Einsicht in Militärregister, Geburts-, Heirats- und Todeslisten sowie US-amerikanische Telefonbücher.
Die Nutzung im Internet ist gebührenpflichtig.

Castle Garden
> www.castlegarden.org
Castle Garden ist die erste offizielle Einwandererstation der USA und Vorläufereinrichtung von Ellis Island. Sie bestand zwischen 1850 und 1890. In der Datenbank sind für die Zeit zwischen 1830 und 1892 über zehn Millionen Einwanderungseinträge gesammelt.
Die Nutzung im Internet ist frei.

Ellis Island Passenger Records
> www.ellisisland.org
2001 wurde im Rahmen der Stiftung „The Statue of Liberty – Ellis Island Foundation, Inc." das „American Family Immigration History Center" gegründet. In diesem Recherchezentrum auf Ellis Island können Besucher in 25 Millionen Datensätzen nach ausgewanderten Vorfahren recherchieren, die zwischen 1892 und 1924 über New York in die USA eingewandert sind.
Die Datenbank steht im Internet frei zur Verfügung, nachdem man sich ein persönliches Passwort eingerichtet hat.

Displaced Persons (DPs) > Englisch für „Heimatlose". Der Fachbegriff wird vor allem in Deutschland für jene etwa sieben Millionen Menschen verwendet, die die westlichen Alliierten im Mai 1945 in ihren Besatzungszonen antrafen. Zwischen 1933 und 1945 aus allen Teilen Europas nach Deutschland verschleppt oder deportiert, konnten oder wollten sie nach Kriegsende nicht mehr in ihre Heimat zurückkehren. Die Zwangsarbeiter und überlebenden KZ-Häftlinge, aber auch Kriegsgefangene und osteuropäische Fremdarbeiter wurden zunächst in DP-Camps in Deutschland untergebracht. Oft nutzte man dafür ehemalige Konzentrationslager, so dass die Menschen unter der täglichen Erinnerung an die grauenvolle Zeit des Holocausts, unter der Enge und Ungewissheit über ihre Zukunft litten. Hunderttausende emigrierten nach Großbritannien, in die USA und nach Kanada. Allein von Bremerhaven fuhren über 800.000 Displaced Persons ab.

E

Einreise- und Aufenthaltsbestimmungen für Argentinien > Die bereits in der ersten Hälfte des 19. Jahrhunderts beginnende staatliche Förderung der europäischen Einwanderung wurde durch die Verfassung von 1853 im Artikel 20 festgelegt. Eine „Masseneinwanderung" erfolgte jedoch erst mit der politischen Stabilisierung des Landes nach 1870. Die Zunahme der sozialistischen und anarchistischen Organisationen und Arbeiterstreiks ab den 1890er Jahren führte 1902 als Reaktion auf den ersten Generalstreik zum Aufenthaltsgesetz („Ley de Residencia"). Dieses ermöglichte, Ausländern die Einreise zu verweigern oder sie auszuweisen, wenn sie als gefährlich für die öffentliche Ordnung betrachtet wurden. Trotz dieser negativen Entwicklungen, für die eingewanderte Arbeiter verantwortlich gemacht wurden, galt die staatliche Förderung der Einwanderung weiterhin als bedeutend.
Erst mit dem Militärputsch gegen Präsident Hipólito Yrigoyen im Jahr 1930 endete die liberale Ära und veränderte die bis dahin weitgehend restriktionsfreie Einwanderungspolitik. Am 1. Januar 1933 trat ein neues Gesetz in Kraft, welches die Einwanderung auf Familiennachzug („llamadas familiares") und Kolonisten in landwirtschaftlichen Ansiedlungen beschränkte. Infolge der Konferenz in Evian wurde in Argentinien am 12. Juli 1938 das „Circular 11" unterzeichnet, eine geheime Direktive, welche die Einwanderung von „Unerwünschten" (vor allem jüdischen Flüchtlingen) nach Argentinien unterbinden sollte.

Einwanderungshäfen > In der Neuen Welt gab es eine Reihe bedeutender Einwanderungshäfen. So war vor allem die Ostküste der USA bevorzugte Anlaufstelle europäischer Einwanderer. Neben New York als größtem Einwanderungshafen der USA gingen über zwei Millionen Menschen in Baltimore von Bord, über eine Million in Philadelphia. Darüber hinaus gehörte Boston ebenso zu den beliebtesten Anlaufstellen wie New Orleans und Galveston im Süden der USA, die vor allem von jenen aufgesucht wurden, die nach Texas weiterreisen wollten. Da der Hafen von Galveston dank seiner Wassertiefe von größeren Schiffen angelaufen werden konnte, löste er ab 1855 New Orleans in seiner Bedeutung ab. Bis 1900 gingen über 100.000 Einwanderer in Galveston an Land, ein Großteil davon Deutsche, die über Bremerhaven gekommen waren. Auch Südamerika lockte Einwanderer an: Zwischen 1850 und 1940 wanderten 6,6 Millionen Europäer in Argentinien ein, die meisten über den Hafen von Buenos Aires. Ein gesuchtes Einwanderungsland war auch Brasilien, dessen Häfen in Rio de Janeiro und Santos zwischen 1819 und 1974 Menschen aus mehr als 50 Nationen aufnahmen, darunter vor allem Italiener, Portugiesen, Spanier und Deutsche. Eine weitere große Einwanderungsstadt war Montevideo in Uruguay, deren Hafen 1868 als fortschrittlichster Umschlagplatz Südamerikas eröffnet wurde.
Für die Einwanderung nach Kanada spielten die Häfen von Quebec und Halifax eine entscheidende Rolle, von denen letzterer zum größten Hafen des Landes wurde. Rund sechs Millionen Menschen gingen über die beiden Häfen an Land.
Zu den klassischen Einwanderungsländern gehörte seit Beginn der Massenauswanderung auch Australien. Hier waren es vor allem die Häfen von Melbourne und Sydney, über die Millionen Einwanderer den fünften Kontinent erreichten.

Ellis Island > Größte Einwanderungsstation der USA. Mit dem starken Ansteigen der Einwanderung vor allem aus Osteuropa ab den 1880er Jahren wurde die Einwanderungsstation **→ Castle Garden** an der Südspitze Manhattans zu klein. Mit der Einführung einheitlicher Einwanderungsbedingungen in den USA wurde 1892 die Einwanderungsstation Ellis Island, eine kleine Insel vor New York, eröffnet.
Die großen Passagierdampfer mit den europäischen Auswanderern an Bord legten zunächst am Pier in Hoboken an, wo die Passagiere der I. und II. Klasse aussteigen konnten. Sie waren bereits an Bord überprüft worden. Die Einwanderer, die in der III. Klasse gereist waren, mussten sich auf Ellis Island dem umfangreichen Einwanderungsverfahren unterziehen: einer Prüfung ihrer Gesundheit sowie einer Befragung durch die Inspektoren der Einwanderungsbehörde. Bis 1954 wurden über 16 Millionen Menschen auf Ellis Island registriert, was die Station zur größten Anlaufstelle der USA machte. Etwa zwei bis drei Prozent der Menschen wurde am Ende der Einwanderungsprozedur die Einreise verweigert. Geschichten über **→ Zurückgewiesene** brachten Ellis Island den Beinamen „Insel der Tränen" ein.

Exil > In der Migrationsforschung wird das Exil, im Unterschied zur Auswanderung, als eine exterritoriale, aber auf die Rückkehr in das Heimatland zielende Form der Wanderung beschrieben. Die USA sind demnach ein Emigrationsland, kein Exilland, denn die vorübergehende Aufnahme von Flüchtlingen aus politischen oder religiösen Gründen ist gesetzlich nicht vorgesehen.

F

Flüchtiger > Im Gegensatz zum Flüchtling die Bezeichnung für eine juristisch verfolgte Person, die sich auf der Flucht befindet. In diese Kategorie fallen beispielsweise die (ehemaligen) deutschen Nationalsozialisten wie Adolf Eichmann, Josef Mengele und Erich Priebke.

Flüchtling > Im Unterschied zu Auswanderern verlassen Flüchtlinge ihr Land unfreiwillig für begrenzte Zeit oder auf Dauer, da sie verfolgt werden oder ihnen Verfolgung droht. Laut **→ Genfer Flüchtlingskonvention** von 1951 gilt als Flüchtling, wer sich aufgrund einer begründeten Furcht vor Verfolgung außerhalb des Staates aufhält, dessen Staatsangehörigkeit er besitzt, oder sich als Staatenloser außerhalb seines gewöhnlichen Aufenthaltsstaates befindet. Anerkannte Verfolgungsgründe sind „Rasse", Religion, Nationalität, Zugehörigkeit zu einer bestimmten sozialen Gruppe und politische Überzeugung.

Freundeskreis
DEUTSCHES AUSWANDERER HAUS e.V.

Freundeskreis Deutsches Auswandererhaus e.V. > Der Freundeskreis ist 2005 aus dem 1985 gegründeten „Förderverein Deutsches Auswanderermuseum e.V." entstanden. Während sich der „Förderverein" 20 Jahre aktiv für die Errichtung eines Auswanderermuseums in Bremerhaven einsetzte, bereichert der Freundeskreis seit der Eröffnung des Deutschen Auswandererhauses im August 2005 das Veranstaltungsprogramm des Hauses durch Vorträge und Informationsveranstaltungen rund um das Thema Migration. Inhaltlich beschäftigen sich die Veranstaltungen vor allem mit den Auswandererhäfen Bremerhaven und Bremen. Die mit über 2.000 Bänden sehr umfangreiche Bibliothek des Freundeskreises zum Thema Migration befindet sich als Dauerleihgabe im Deutschen Auswandererhaus.

G

Genealogie > Sie beschäftigt sich mit der Abstammung von Menschen, sowohl in aufsteigender (Vorfahren) als auch absteigender Linie (Nachfahren). Sobald die Forschung über rein biologische Zusammenhänge hinausgeht, spricht man von Familienforschung. Volkstümlich wird die Genealogie auch Ahnenforschung genannt.

Genfer Flüchtlingskonvention > Ziel der „Genfer Flüchtlingskonvention", die im Juli 1951 auf einer UN-Sonderkonferenz verabschiedet wurde, ist es, einen einheitlichen Rechtsstatus für **→ Flüchtlinge** zu schaffen, die keinen diplomatischen Schutz ihres Heimatlandes genießen. Die 146 Vertragsstaaten verpflichten sich unter anderem, Flüchtlingen **→ Asyl** zu gewähren. Die „Genfer Flüchtlingskonvention" und das Protokoll von 1967 die Rechtsgrundlage für das „Amt des Hohen Flüchtlingskommissars der Vereinten Nationen" (UNHCR).

Globalisierung > Die zunehmende weltweite Vernetzung der Menschen und Gesellschaften wirkt sich sowohl auf wirtschaftliche Beziehungen (z. B. Firmenzusammenschlüsse) als auch auf den privaten Bereich (z. B. Internet) aus. Globalisierungskritiker weisen darauf hin, dass durch die Globalisierung Arbeitsplätze in Länder mit geringem Lohnniveau transferiert werden; vor allem Großunternehmen in den reichen Ländern profitieren, während Länder mit geringerer Wirtschaftskraft verlieren. Befürworter sehen in den zusammenwachsenden Märkten und Gesellschaften die Möglichkeiten für wirtschaftliche und soziale Vereinigungen auf den unterschiedlichsten Ebenen.

H

Hapag / Hapag-Lloyd > Ausgelöst durch die rasch wachsende Bedeutung Bremerhavens als Auswandererhafen wurde 1847 in Hamburg die „Hamburg-Amerikanische Packetfahrt-Actien-Gesellschaft" (Hapag) gegründet. Ziel war es, mit einer direkten Segelschiff-Verbindung von Hamburg nach Nordamerika am Geschäft mit der Beförderung von Auswanderern teilzunehmen. Hatte der **→ Norddeutsche Lloyd** (NDL) von Beginn an auf Dampfschiffe gesetzt, führte die Hapag erst 1889 Schnelldampfer ein. Gleichzeitig bot die Reederei Kreuzfahrten für Urlauber an. 1901 eröffnete die Hapag in Hamburg die Auswandererstadt, die bis zu 5.000 Menschen beherbergen konnte (siehe

auch → **Veddel**). Sowohl nach dem Ersten als auch nach dem Zweiten Weltkrieg verloren die Hapag und der NDL ihre gesamte Flotte, die als Reparationszahlung an die Alliierten ging. Beim Wiederaufbau der Flotten und Liniendienste ab 1954 kooperierten beide Reedereien, um eine Konkurrenz zu vermeiden. 1970 fusionierte die Hapag mit dem NDL zur „Hapag-Lloyd AG". Bedeutende Schiffe der Hapag: die „Augusta Victoria" (1889), die „Fürst Bismarck" (1891), das damals schnellste Schiff auf der Nordamerika-Linie. Die „Deutschland" errang auf der Jungfernreise 1900 das → **Blaue Band**, der „Imperator" (1913) und der „Vaterland" (1914) waren beide die größten Schiffe ihrer Zeit.

Heimat > Heimat ist für viele Menschen ein geographischer Ort, mit dem sie sich sehr verbunden fühlen, den sie als Zuhause empfinden, an dem sie sich nicht erklären müssen. Heimat steht damit im Gegensatz zu Fremde und Exil. Heimat ist häufig, aber nicht unbedingt der Ort, an dem man geboren ist (Wahlheimat). Im Englischen lässt sich Heimat mit „homeland" oder „native land" übersetzen.
Das Wort Heimat hat seinen Ursprung in der Romantik. In Deutschland ist der Begriff umstritten, weil er für viele durch die historische Entwicklung einen völkischen und nationalen Beiklang hat.

Hyphen-Americans > (dt.: „Bindestrich-Amerikaner") Viele ethnische Gruppierungen in den USA verspüren trotz ihrer amerikanischen Staatsbürgerschaft eine starke Verbundenheit mit ihrem Herkunftsland und halten kulturelle Traditionen und Gewohnheiten aufrecht. Italian-Americans, African-Americans, Polish-Americans und andere Hyphen-Americans sind den USA gegenüber sehr loyal, definieren ihre Staatsbürgerschaft als primär politisch und empfinden sich als Mitglied der amerikanischen Einwanderungsgesellschaft.

I

IMIS – Institut für Migrationsforschung und Interkulturelle Studien > Das interdisziplinäre und interfakultative Forschungsinstitut der Universität Osnabrück beschäftigt sich mit historischen und gegenwärtigen Migrationsbewegungen sowie mit politischen, sozialen und kulturellen Aspekten der Migration und Integration.
> www.imis.uni-osnabrueck.de

Integration
→ **Akkulturation / Assimilation**

K

Kai / Kaje > Kaje und Kai sind Begriffe für ein durch Mauern befestigtes Ufer. Der Begriff Kaje stammt aus dem Niederländischen. Er wird in der Region um Bremerhaven, aber auch in anderen deutschen Küstenregionen verwendet. Die Kaje hat den Wasserzugang auf einer Seite – im Gegensatz zum Pier, das beidseitig einen Wasserzugang hat.

Kettenwanderung > Berichte von geglückten Neuanfängen vieler Auswanderer gelangten durch Briefe und Zeitungsartikel in die alte Heimat. Ermuntert von ausgewanderten Familienmitgliedern und Bekannten folgten Hunderttausende nach. Vielerorts, etwa in Preußen, Mecklenburg oder Württemberg kam es durch Kettenwanderungen in einer Reihe von Ortschaften zu erheblichen Bevölkerungsrückgängen.
Das große Ansteigen der Auswandererzahlen aus Europa in der zweiten Hälfte des 19. Jahrhunderts wird unter anderem auf die „Multiplikator-Effekte" der Kettenwanderung zurückgeführt, die sich bis zu Beginn des 20. Jahrhunderts zu dem am weitesten verbreiteten Auswanderungsmuster entwickelte.

L

Luftverkehr > In den 1960er Jahren verlor das Geschäft mit der Auswanderung per Schiff an Bedeutung. Bremerhaven und Hamburg hatten als Auswandererhäfen ausgedient. Ein zentraler Grund dafür ist neben den nordamerikanischen Einwanderungsbeschränkungen die Möglichkeit, seit Ende der 1950er Jahre den Atlantik per Flugzeug in wesentlich kürzerer Zeit zu überqueren.
Die „Deutsche Lufthansa AG" als staatliche Fluggesellschaft wurde 1926 durch einen Zusammenschluss der „Deutschen Aero Lloyd" mit dem „Junkers Luftverkehr" gegründet. Nach dem Zweiten Weltkrieg erfolgte 1955 die Neugründung der Lufthansa. Zwischen 1994 und 1997 wurde die Fluglinie komplett privatisiert.

M

Meier, Hermann Heinrich > Der Bremer Geschäftsmann und Politiker (1809–1898) gründete 1857 den → **Norddeutschen Lloyd**, der sich zu einer der größten Reedereien weltweit entwickelte.

Melting Pot / Salad Bowl > Die USA wurden in der Soziologie lange Zeit als „Melting Pot" beschrieben, als „Schmelztiegel", in dem sich die verschiedenen ethnischen Herkünfte seiner Einwanderer zu einer neuen eigenständigen Kultur vermischen. Diese Sichtweise wird jedoch zunehmend berichtigt. An ihre Stelle tritt das multikulturelle Konzept der „Salatschüssel" („Salad Bowl") als nicht homogene, aber in sich strukturierte und harmonierende Einheit.

Migration > Wanderungsbewegungen von Einzelnen oder Gruppen, die mit einem kurzfristigen, längerfristigen oder dauerhaften Wohnortwechsel verbunden sind. Man unterscheidet zwischen Emigration (Auswanderung) und Immigration (Einwanderung). Bei Wohnortwechseln innerhalb eines Staates spricht man von Binnenwanderung, das Durchqueren von Staaten bezeichnet man als Transitwanderung.
Die Gründe und der Grad der Freiwilligkeit der jeweiligen Emigration sind sehr unterschiedlich, darum unterscheidet man bei Migranten zwischen → **Auswanderern**, → **Arbeitsmigranten**, → **Flüchtlingen** und → **Vertriebenen**.

Missler-Hallen > Um das Unterbringungsproblem der in Bremen auf ihre Abfahrt nach Bremerhaven wartenden Auswanderer zu lösen, ließen der → **Norddeutsche Lloyd** und sein Hauptagent Friedrich Missler 1906/1907 im Bremer Stadtteil Findorff Auswandererhallen errichten. Sie sollten insbesondere den Ost- und Südosteuropäern ausreichendes und billiges Quartier bieten. Das Modell Auswandererhallen hatte sich bereits in Hamburg auf der Veddel bewährt.

Staatsarchiv Bremen

Sammlung Deutsches Auswandererhaus / Collection German Emigration Center

Links: „Missler-Hallen" im Bremer Stadtteil Findorff, um 1911. Rechts: Dokumententasche des Auswandereragenten Friedrich Missler, um 1920. / Left: *Missler Halls* in Findorff, a district of Bremen, about 1911. Right: Emigration agent Friedrich Missler's document case, about 1920.

1907 wurden die neuen – im Volksmund „Missler-Hallen" genannten – Quartiere mit Platz für mehr als 2.700 Menschen fertiggestellt. Nach dem Tod Misslers 1922 übernahm der „Norddeutsche Lloyd" die Gebäude, nun „Lloydheim" genannt, für die Betreuung seiner Fahrgäste.

N

New Immigrants > (dt.: Neue Einwanderer) Um die Jahrhundertwende kamen immer mehr süd- und osteuropäische Auswanderer nach Amerika: vorwiegend Italiener, Griechen sowie Katholiken und Juden aus Osteuropa. Erstmals im Jahre 1896 überstieg ihre Anzahl die der „alten Einwanderer" aus nord- und nordwesteuropäischen Ländern. Viele Amerikaner beobachteten diese Entwicklung kritisch, die „New Immigrants" wurden als Bedrohung für die amerikanische Gesellschaft angesehen und marginalisiert. Es folgte eine lebhafte Diskussion um Einwanderungsbeschränkungen, die letzlich im **→ Quota Act** von 1921 mündete, der die gesamte Einwanderung nach einem Quotensystem regelte, bei dem die ost- und südosteuropäischen Einwanderer benachteiligt waren.

Norddeutscher Lloyd (NDL) > Die 1857 in Bremen gegründete Dampfschifffahrtsgesellschaft war die erste Reederei, die einen regelmäßigen Schiffsverkehr zwischen Deutschland und New York aufbaute. Im Deutschen Kaiserreich (1871–1918) stieg der NDL zu einer der größten Reedereien der Welt auf. Seine Schiffe befuhren Routen in die USA, nach Südamerika und Australien. Die meisten Passagiere waren Auswanderer, aber auch amerikanische und deutsche Touristen reisten auf Schiffen des NDL.
Heimathafen der Bremer Reederei war Bremerhaven. 1869 eröffnete sie am „Neuen Hafen" die erste Wartehalle, die zweite Wartehalle folgte 1897 an der Kaiserschleuse. Da die Bremerhavener Hafen- und Schleusenanlagen für die immer größer werdenden Schiffe zu klein wurden, fuhren die Schiffe des NDL zwischen 1890 und 1896 von Nordenham ab, das am westlichen Weserufer gegenüber von Bremerhaven liegt. Aus der ersten Werkstatt des NDL, in der die Schiffe gewartet und repariert werden konnten, entwickelte sich die „Lloyd Werft Bremerhaven", die bis heute existiert und in den Bereichen Schiffsverlängerung und Umbau zu den bekanntesten Werften zählt. Zu den berühmtesten Schiffen des NDL gehörten der erste Vierschornsteindampfer „Kaiser Wilhelm der Große", die „Columbus", die „Europa" und die „Bremen", die 1929 das **→ Blaue Band** für die schnellste Atlantiküberquerung errang. 1970 fusionierten der NDL und die Hapag, einst größte Konkurrenten des Passagierverkehrs auf See, zur **→ Hapag-Lloyd**.

Sammlung Deutsches Auswandererhaus / Collection German Emigration Center

Passagierliste der „Seydlitz" von ihrer Fahrt von Bremerhaven nach New York, 17.03.1923. / Passenger list of the *Seydlitz* en route from Bremerhaven to New York, 17 March 1923.

P

Pilgrim Fathers > (dt.: „Pilgerväter") Als religiöse Separatisten in England verfolgt, wanderten die puritanischen Pilgerväter im 17. Jahrhundert nach Amerika aus. Sie waren die ersten englischen Siedler in Neuengland.
Legendär ist die Geschichte der „Mayflower". Im Jahre 1602 brachte das Segelschiff 102 Menschen, vorwiegend Pilgrims, nach Amerika. Die Überfahrt von Plymouth (England) nach Plymouth (Massachusetts) dauerte vom 16. September bis zum 11. November.

Pogrom > Im weiteren Sinne bezeichnet Pogrom (russ.: Verwüstung, Zerstörung, Krawall) Ausschreitungen gegenüber religiösen, nationalen und ethnischen Minderheiten. Eng verbunden ist der Begriff mit antijüdischen Gewalttaten und Plünderungen. Im zaristischen Russland lösten wiederholte Pogrome zwischen 1880 und 1913 große Auswanderungswellen russischer Juden in die USA und nach Palästina aus. Im nationalsozialistischen Deutschland wurden die antijüdischen Novemberpogrome 1938 von staatlicher Seite initiiert. Das letzte große Pogrom gegen Juden in Europa fand 1946 im polnischen Kielce statt.

Q

Quota Act > Mit dem „Emergency Quota Act" vom 19. Mai 1921 schränkten die USA die jährliche Zuwanderung massiv ein und bevorzugten Einwanderer aus Nord- und Westeuropa. Jährlich war nur noch eine Zuwanderung von drei Prozent jeder 1910 in den USA lebenden Herkunftsnationalität erlaubt: den Census-Daten nach insgesamt 357.802 Einwanderer, von denen mehr als die Hälfte aus nord- und westeuropäischen Ländern stammte. Für Einwanderer aus Süd- und Osteuropa bedeutetete der „Quota Act" eine Reduktion um 75 Prozent im Vergleich zu den Vorjahren. In dem an der Herkunftsnation orientierten Quotensystem schlug sich die seit Jahrzehnten zunehmende Fremdenangst nieder. Die USA verschärften 1924 mit dem „National Origins Act" – insgesamt 164.000 Zuwanderer jährlich bei maximal zwei Prozent aus jeder Herkunftsnationalität von 1890 – ihre restriktive Einwanderungspolitik noch weiter.

R

Raphaels-Werk > Bis heute ist der 1871 gegründete christliche Verein zum Schutz katholischer Auswanderer – benannt nach dem Erzengel Raphael, der als Beschützer der Reisenden verehrt wird – eine Beratungsstelle für Menschen, die Deutschland vorübergehend oder dauerhaft verlassen wollen. Auch die zur Diakonie gehörende „Evangelische Auswandererberatung e. V." (heute Auslandsberatung) bot Auswanderungswilligen Beratung an.
> www.raphaels-werk.de
> www.ev-auslandsberatung.de

Rattenlinie > (engl.: ratline) Vom US-amerikanischen Geheimdienst geprägter Begriff, der den Fluchtweg führender Vertreter des NS-Regimes nach dem Ende des Zweiten Weltkrieges beschreibt. Die Route führte über Italien, Süditalien oder auch Rom, nach Südamerika – dort insbesondere nach Argentinien. Auf diese Weise entkamen viele Nazis zunächst ihrer Strafe für die begangenen Verbrechen während der nationalsozialistischen Diktatur in Deutschland (1933–1945).

S

Sammlung Deutsches Auswandererhaus > In den vergangenen vier Jahren hat unsere Sammlung einen Umfang von mehr als 2.800 Objekten angenommen. Hauptsächlich setzt sich diese beachtliche Zahl aus Fotos und Briefen zusammen. Aber auch Gepäckstücke, Passagierlisten, Reisepässe, Andenken von Schiffspassagen oder persönliche Dokumente sind wichtiger Bestandteil unseres Archivs. Meist sind es Besucher, die nach dem Rundgang an uns herantreten, denen während des Aufenthaltes ein verborgener Schatz auf dem Dachboden wieder einfällt oder die sich an einen längst vergessenen Teil ihrer Familiengeschichte erinnern. So gelangen die spannenden Geschichte von „Abenteurern" in unsere Hände. Doch nicht allein der abstrakte Lebenslauf eines Auswanderers interessiert uns. Es sind vielmehr die dazugehörigen Objekte, die das Leben eben jenes Migranten für uns und unsere Besucher so anschaulich werden lassen. In unserer Ausstellung geht es deshalb immer um die Verbindung zwischen Objekt und Lebensgeschichte. Ohne das jeweils Andere wäre unser Museum nicht so ausdrucksstark und lebendig.

St. Raphaels-Blatt

Organ des St. Raphaels-Vereins zum Schutze katholischer deutscher Auswanderer.

Das St. Raphaels-Blatt erscheint 4 Mal im Jahre, jeden ersten Monat des Quartals, und kostet, durch die Post bezogen, 1 Mark pro Jahr.

1. Jahrgang. № 4. Oktober 1886.

Inhalt: Der St. Raphaels-Verein und die Auswanderung. Rede des Herrn Pastor P. Schlösser auf der XXXIII. General-Versammlung deutscher Katholiken zu Breslau. — Fürsorge für die deutschen Auswanderer. — Zur Auswanderung nach Südbrasilien. — Vermischtes. — St. Raphaels-Verein (1886).

Der St. Raphaels-Verein und die Auswanderung.
Rede des Herrn Pastor P. Schlösser
auf der XXXIII. Generalversammlung deutscher Katholiken zu Breslau.

In der Geschichte der neueren Zeit begegnen wir einer Erscheinung, welche nun fast ein halbes Jahrhundert lang allseitige Aufmerksamkeit erregt und zwar darum, weil sie in unsere sozial-politischen Verhältnisse tief eingreift und nicht minder eine hohe religiös-sittliche Bedeutung hat: es ist die Auswanderung aus der alten in die neue Welt. Seit Mitte der dreißiger Jahre sehen wir in ununterbrochener Reihenfolge jedes Jahr Tausende unserer deutschen Mitbürger den heimathlichen Heerd verlassen, um sich jenseits des Ozeans

Raphaels-Werk e.V., Hamburg

Das „St. Raphaels-Blatt" vom Oktober 1886 informiert u. a. über die Auswanderung nach Brasilien. / The October 1886 edition of *St. Raphaels-Blatt* (bulletin published by German organization *Raphaels-Werk*) provides information on emigration to Brazil.

S.Volk / Collection German Emigration Center

Sammlungsleiterin Katrin Quirin sichtet und inventarisiert neu eingegangene Schenkungen. / Katrin Quirin, the collection curator, oversees and inventories newly acquired donations.

Schiffsklassen > Die technische Entwicklung der Schiffe veränderte die Überfahrtsbedingungen der Auswanderer erheblich – vor allem für Passagiere der III. Klasse: Auf den Segelschiffen waren sie meist zu Hunderten in stickigen und engen Zwischendecks untergebracht, in denen katastrophale hygienische Zustände herrschten. Viele Menschen fanden auf der bis zu 15 Wochen dauernden Atlantiküberfahrt den Tod. Mit Einführung der Schnelldampfer ab 1880 verringerte sich die Reisedauer nach Amerika auf acht bis 15 Tage. Passagieren der III. Klasse standen zudem Neuerungen wie Sanitäranlagen zur Verfügung. Dank größerer Maschinen und verbesserter Antriebstechnik bewältigten die vom **→ Norddeutschen Lloyd** ab 1897 eingesetzten Liner die Atlantiküberquerung in sechs Tagen. Diese Schiffe waren erheblich sicherer. Sie boten den III. Klasse-Passagieren ab 1906 einen eigenen Speisesaal. Ab Ende der 1920er Jahre ersetzten Mehrbettkabinen die Massenunterkünfte, zusätzlich wurde eine Touristenklasse eingeführt.

Stiftung Deutsches Auswandererhaus > Das Deutsche Auswandererhaus Bremerhaven ist ein Public-Private-Partnership-Projekt, das aus öffentlichen Mitteln errichtet wurde und seit seiner Eröffnung im August 2005 privat betrieben wird. Um aufwändige und umfangreiche Projekte zu unterstützen und die Ziele des Deutschen Auswandererhauses international zu verankern, wurde im Januar 2006 die Stiftung Deutsches Auswandererhaus gegründet.

Auch sie ist ein Public-Private-Partnership-Projekt, das vom „Initiativkreis Erlebniswelt Auswanderung Bremerhaven e. V.", Vertretern der Bremerhavener Wirtschaft, der Stadt Bremerhaven und der Betreibergesellschaft des Deutschen Auswandererhauses gegründet wurde.

Die Stiftung soll das Haus in die Lage versetzen, die Geschichte der Auswanderung in ihrer historischen und aktuellen Bedeutung für Deutschland, Europa, die Vereinigten Staaten von Amerika wie die übrigen Aufnahmeländer umfassend zu erforschen und durch Ausstellungen und Publikationen einer breiten Öffentlichkeit im In- und Ausland zu vermitteln. So sieht der Stiftungszweck vor, Exponate und Sammlungen zum Thema zu erwerben und den wissenschaftlichen Aufbau wie die Pflege der Datenbank und einer Archivbibliothek zu unterstützen. Darüber hinaus wird die Stiftung Projekte, Tagungen und Sonderveranstaltungen fördern, die sich mit der Thematik des Hauses – die Migration des 19. und 20. Jahrhunderts und aktuelle Migrationsbewegungen – befassen. Der Austausch von Studenten aus den europäischen Nachbarländern und Übersee und die Vergabe von Forschungsstipendien sind weitere Aufgaben der Stiftung, um die Inhalte des Deutschen Auswandererhauses auch wissenschaftlich zu verankern.

> www.stiftung-dah.org

Stiftung DEUTSCHES AUSWANDERER HAUS

T

Transitwanderung > Ende des 19. Jahrhunderts und in der Zeit der Weimarer Republik (1919–1933) durchquerten viele Auswanderer aus Süd- und Osteuropa das Gebiet des Deutschen Reichs, um von Hamburg oder Bremerhaven aus die Fahrt über den Atlantik anzutreten.

V

Veddel > Um den immer größer werdenden Strom der Auswanderer am Stadtzentrum vorbeizuleiten, ließ die Hamburger Reederei **→ Hapag** ab 1898 auf der zwischen Norder- und Süderelbe gelegenen Insel Veddel Auswandererhallen errichten. 1901 eröffnet, wurde die Unterkunft stetig erweitert und umfasste letztlich ein Areal von 55.000 Quadratmetern mit rund 30 Einzelgebäuden.

Die dezentrale Lage sowie für damalige Zeit vorbildliche hygienische Bedingungen resultierten daraus, dass man russische Auswanderer für den Ausbruch der Cholera-Epidemie von 1892 verantwortlich machte. Auf der Veddel wurde jeder ankommende Auswanderer zunächst einer Gesundheitsprüfung unterzogen und blieb bis zu 14 Tage in Quarantäne. Zugleich verhinderte man, dass mittellose Auswanderer ins Stadtzentrum gelangten.

Neben Schlaf- und Wohnpavillons umfasste die Anlage einen großen Speisesaal, Bäder und eine Desinfektionsanstalt. Auch eine Kirche für beide christlichen Konfessionen und eine Synagoge standen den Auswanderern zur Verfügung. Nach der Erweiterung 1906/1907 wurden jüdische und christliche Auswanderer in separaten Küchen und Speisesälen versorgt. Während des Ersten Weltkrieges dienten die Auswandererhallen als Lazarett. Zwischenzeitlich wieder für Auswanderer geöffnet, wurden die Auswandererhallen 1934 von der SS in Besitz genommen. Vorher wanderten vor allem jüdische Flüchtlinge über Hamburg nach Amerika aus. Die Hallen wurden später als Lager genutzt und größtenteils abgerissen. Im Juli 2007 wurde hier unter dem Namen „BallinStadt" ein Museum eröffnet.

Vertreibung / Vertriebene > Vertreibung ist eine erzwungene Auswanderung einzelner Personen oder ganzer ethnischer Gruppen aus von ihnen besiedelten Gebieten. Nach dem Zweiten Weltkrieg wurden Deutsche aus den ehemaligen Ostprovinzen und den deutschen Siedlungsgebieten in Ost- und Südosteuropa vertrieben. Schon vor Kriegsende beschlossen die Alliierten die Rückführung der deutschen Minderheiten, um zukünftige kulturelle und ethnische Konflikte zu verhindern. Siehe auch **→ Aussiedler / Spätaussiedler**

Visum > Eine behördliche Erlaubnis zum Überschreiten der Grenze eines Landes. Der Erhalt eines Visums war und ist Voraussetzung für die Einwanderung und Teil des Einwanderungsverfahrens.

W

White Star Line > Im Zuge des australischen Goldrausches wurde 1845 die „Aberdeen White Star Line" gegründet, um Gold und andere Waren aus Australien nach Europa zu bringen. Den Durchbruch im transatlantischen Geschäft erlebte die Reederei erst, nachdem sie von hölzernen Segel-

schiffen auf eiserne Dampfer umstieg. Mehrere Schiffe gewannen das → **Blaue Band** (unter anderem die „Adreatic" 1872, „Germanic" 1875, „Teutonic" und „Majestic" 1891), bis ein neuer Eigner auf Größe und Luxus statt auf Geschwindigkeit setzte. Nach dem Verlust der beiden bekanntesten Schiffe, der „Titanic" und des Schwesternschiffes „Britannic", stand die „White Star Line" immer wieder vor dem Ruin und wurde schließlich mit der → **Cunard Line** zur „Cunard White Star Line" vereint.

Wolgadeutsche > Diese Sammelbezeichnung fasst deutsche Bevölkerungsgruppen aus dem Wolga- und Schwarzmeergebiet zusammen. Die russische Zarin Katharina die Große rief 1762/1763 deutsche Kolonisten zur Landbesiedlung nach Russland. Allein bis 1864 wurden über 300 Kolonien gegründet. Durch die Reformen Alexanders II. verloren die Kolonisten seit 1871 einen Großteil ihrer Sonderrechte. Dies veranlasste eine größere Anzahl zur Auswanderung auch nach Nord- und Südamerika. Die Aufrechterhaltung ihrer kulturellen (und sprachlichen) Eigenständigkeit gehörte zu den Motiven ihrer Auswanderung.

Y

Yerba > ist der Hauptbestandteil des argentinischen Nationalgetränks, des Mate-Tees. Das Wort Mate geht im Ursprung auf die indigene Bezeichnung für das traditionell aus Kürbisschale bestehende Trinkgefäß zurück. Der aus dem Spanischen abgeleitete Begriff Yerba meint dagegen das Teekraut selbst.

Z

Zech, Paul (1881–1946) > gehört zu den vielseitigsten und schaffensreichsten deutschen Schriftstellern des frühen 20. Jahrhunderts. Als SPD-Sympathisant geriet er 1933 ins Visier des NS-Regimes und verließ nach einer kurzen Inhaftierung Deutschland. Sein Fluchtweg führte ihn ins argentinische Exil, wo er 1946 auch verstarb. Seine während des Aufenthalts in Südamerika (1933–1946) entstandenen Werke sind der deutschen Exilliteratur zuzuordnen.

Zurückgewiesene > Nicht jeder Passagier, der die Neue Welt erreichte, durfte auch tatsächlich einreisen. In einem Einwanderungsverfahren legten die aufnehmenden Staaten fest, welche Bedingungen erfüllt werden mussten. Meist führten bestimmte Krankheiten, körperliche oder geistige Behinderungen sowie fehlende Bürgschaften oder eine kriminelle Vorgeschichte des Antragstellers zu einer Ablehnung. In allen Fällen wurden die Kosten für die Rückreise der jeweiligen Reederei auferlegt. Kinder ab zehn Jahren mussten allein zurückreisen, wenn der Rest der Familie aufgenommen wurde. Die Ablehnungsquote war allerdings recht gering. So betrug sie etwa in New York auf der Einwandererstation Ellis Island nur zwei bis drei Prozent.

GLOSSARY

A

Acculturation / Assimilation > Acculturation is a term used in migration research referring to the various processes of integration in immigrant societies. Ethnologists, sociologists and historians alike use this word to denote the assimilation and adaptation of various cultures in one common society. Immigrants and local citizens experience mutual cultural exchange and interchange in the country of assimilation. Completion of this process may involve several generations and thus decades. The first step in this exchange involves the acceptance or tolerance of eating habits, and religious and political holidays. Immigrants have different strategies according to individual preference. Whereas some wish to become integrated and accepted in the society of assimilation as quickly as possible, others tend to separate or isolate themselves from the members of the host society. Ideally, integration takes place while maintaining one's cultural roots. The success or failure of the integration process depends on the society and politics of the country of assimilation.
The term assimilation is considered outdated in modern migration research as it denotes the abandonment of the immigrant's original cultural identity. Studies in various countries of immigration such as the U.S.A., but also Germany, have shown that the concept of immigrants dispensing with their original cultural background after migrating to a new country is wrong.
See also → **Melting pot / Salad bowl**

AEMI—The Association of European Migration Institutions > A cooperation forum of European institutions and organizations which focuses on historic and current migration, organizes international symposia and joint research projects.
> www.aemi.dk

Air travel > When the heyday of ocean-going vessels as a form of emigrant transportation receded in the 1960s, Bremerhaven and Hamburg lost their importance as major ports of emigration. In addition to the tightening of U.S. immigration restrictions, transatlantic crossings had become easier and faster with the introduction of air travel. In 1926, *Deutsche Aero Lloyd* and *Junkers Luftverkehr* merged to create the German national airline *Deutsche Lufthansa AG*. After the Second World War *Lufthansa* was newly founded in 1955. The airline underwent complete privatization between 1994 and 1997.

Asylum > For centuries free states, hospices, convents and monasteries have granted sanctuary to those in need of protection due to persecution. Today, asylum has come to mean the recognition of political refugees. Pursuant to Article 16 of the German Constitution every person has a right to political asylum. This right of asylum, the freest anywhere in the world, was greatly amended in 1993. As a result, virtually no one from a country "free of persecution" or anyone entering the Federal Republic of Germany by way of "a third, safe country" has a right to asylum. During the court hearing determining a person's right to political asylum, which may last anywhere from two weeks to several years, asylum seekers must live in designated accommodations and may not leave their place of residence without prior approval. Social benefits are reduced and in some German federal states asylum seekers receive food stamps or food packages

instead of money. Since 2001, asylum seekers and tolerated foreigners are allowed to work provided the job cannot be filled by a German national or a foreign resident with a residence permit. Those entitled to political asylum first receive a temporary residence permit for three years. If this is not revoked they then receive a permanent residence permit.

Aussiedler / Spätaussiedler > So-called *Aussiedler* are people of German extraction who have moved back to Germany from East and Southeast Europe, where their families have sometimes been living for generations, notably from the Middle Ages up until the nineteenth century, following a call by the Russian czars for laborers, craftsmen and settlers. Since 1950 over four million *Aussiedler* have "returned" to Germany, mainly from the Soviet Union and CIS countries. Pursuant to the *Federal Eviction and Refugee Act* of 1953 they were entitled to German citizenship, and their integration in the population promoted. As of 1993, *Aussiedler* from countries outside the CIS are only recognized if they are able to provide proof of discrimination due to their ethnic German origin. In addition, only *Spätaussiedler* are entitled to apply for German citizenship if born prior to 1993. In 1996, a further obstacle was introduced, a language test, which is also mandatory for members of the family traveling with the person involved who are not of German descent.

B

Ballin, Albert > The youngest son of a Jewish merchant (1857–1918) who began his career with **→ Hapag** in the year 1886. The Hamburg shipping line was quick to assign managerial tasks to this young employee. By 1888 Ballin had risen to an executive position, in 1899 he became the managing director of Hapag. Ballin contributed enormously to Hamburg's rise as a port of emigration. See also **→ Veddel**

Bandoneon (-ion) > The bandoneon, a type of accordion, is part of the concertina family of instruments. German sailors and emigrants to Argentina brought the instrument with them in the 1870s where it soon played an essential role in the tango orchestra.

Belgranodeutsch > A mixture of German and Spanish originally spoken by German emigrants who settled predominantly in the district by the same name and still spoken today by the German community living in the Belgrano neighborhood of Buenos Aires.

Blue Ribbon > Winning the *Blue Ribbon* for the fastest transatlantic crossing was in the age of the steamship a major honor for shipping companies. The *Sirius* was the first steamer to receive this award in 1838. Up until the turn of the century English ships had dominated this field, then the era of the great ships of the **→ North German Lloyd** (*Norddeutscher Lloyd*) and **→ Hapag** shipping lines dawned. The last great steamship to win the *Blue Ribbon* was the *United States* in 1952.

Bremen Decree > The first government-enforced regulation designed to protect emigrants in Germany. The Bremen Decree of 1832 was crucial in promoting Bremerhaven's good reputation as a port of emigration. Shipping lines were now legally obligated to document the seaworthiness of their ships, carry sufficient provisions and maintain minimal standards for passengers on board.

C

Castle Garden > America's first receiving station. As a central point of arrival Castle Garden offered incoming immigrants protection from profiteers and the opportunity to purchase train tickets for their journey inland. Here, too, immigrants were registered in individual ship manifests. These passenger records, known as "manifests," are valuable documents for family and genealogical researchers the world over. (**→ Databases / Family research**). An estimated eight million immigrants entered America by way of Castle Garden between 1855 and 1890. Castle Garden was later replaced by **→ Ellis Island**.

Chain Migration > Emigrants who reported back home of successful new lives or sent letters and clippings from the New World encouraged hundreds of thousands of friends and relatives to follow in their footsteps. In many towns and areas, particularly in Prussia, Mecklenburg and Württemberg chain migration caused the population to drop drastically.
Invariably the phenomenal increase in emigrants

Sammlung Deutsches Auswandererhaus / Collection German Emigration Center

Fotopostkarte der „Bremen" an der Columbuskaje in Bremerhaven. Der Dampfer bekam auf seiner Jungfernfahrt von Bremerhaven nach New York im Jahr 1929 das „Blaue Band" für die schnellste Antlantiküberquerung. / Photo postcard of the *Bremen* anchored at the Columbus wharf in Bremerhaven. The steamer received the *Blue Ribbon* for the fastest transatlantic crossing on its maiden voyage from Bremerhaven to New York in 1929.

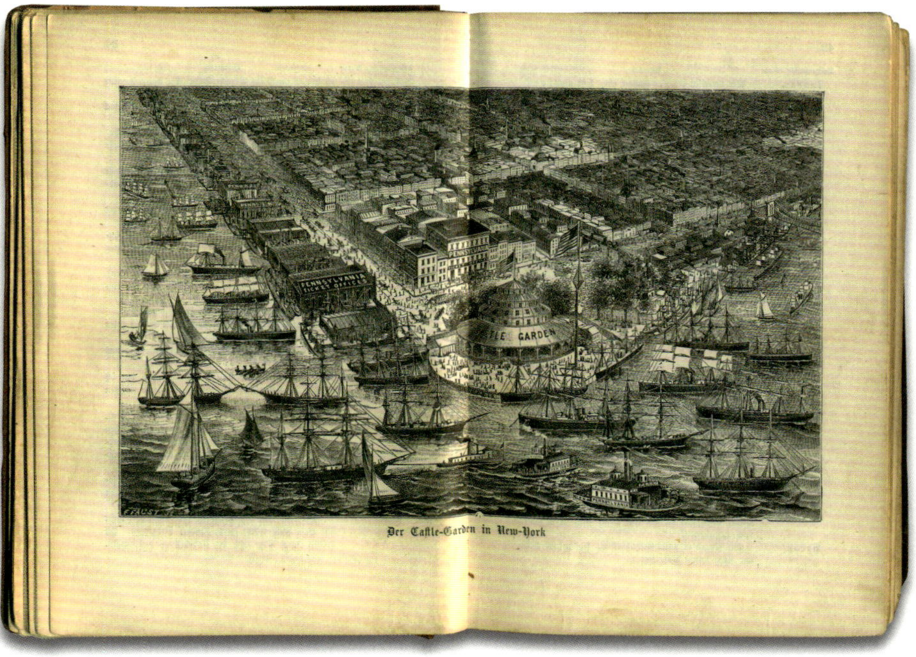

Sammlung Deutsches Auswandererhaus / Collection German Emigration Center

Castle Garden in New York. Aus: Adolf Ott: „Der Führer nach Amerika", 1882. / Castle Garden in New York. Excerpt from Adolf Ott: *Der Führer nach Amerika* (The Guidebook to America), 1882.

from Europe during the latter half of the nineteenth century and continuing up through the early twentieth century is attributed to the multiplier effect of chain reaction emigration and represents the most widespread pattern of emigration there has ever been.

Collection German Emigration Center > In the last four years our collection has grown to more than 2,800 exhibits, consisting to a great extent of photos and letters. However, there are also pieces of luggage, passenger lists, passports, souvenirs and personal documents which make up a significant part of our archive.
In most cases, visitors who have toured the museum come to us afterwards having remembered a forgotten memento or treasure in their attic at home or who recall a long-forgotten part of their family story. That is how we come to possess the exciting stories of all these "adventurers." We are not only interested in the abstract vita of an emigrant, but rather in the many objects which formed a part of a migrant's life and make these individual fates come alive for our visitors. That is why our exhibition combines display object and life story. The one without the other would make our museum far less expressive and vivid.

Colonia Liebig > Located in the northern part of the Corrientes province in Argentina. On 27 January 1924, the German-South American colony and cooperative *Neu Karlsruhe*, as the town was first named, was founded. When this settlement project, originally planned for Paraguay, failed, the first two to three hundred German settlers obtained land in Corrientes from the Liebig Company (*Liebig Extract of Meat Company*) which gave the colony its name. The founding of the *Cooperativa Agrícola de la Colonia Liebig* followed in December 1926, Walter Ostermann was the company's first president. To this day, the cooperative produces mate tea.

Cunard Line > The *British and North American Royal Mail Steam Packet Company* (renamed in 1878), formed by the Canadian Samuel Cunard in 1839 as a reliable mail service between Great Britain and North America. The first four steamships were put into service as early as 1840 and a regular weekly mail service set up from Liverpool to Halifax and Boston. Passengers were welcome to travel on these steamships from the start. The *Cunard Line* dominated mail and passenger transport service up through 1870, yet suffered from the very demanding conditions made by the line´s financial backers.

Hurt by the Great Depression and under pressure from the British government, the *Cunard Line* merged with the → **White Star Line** in 1932, thus becoming the *Cunard White Star Line* and focusing increasingly on passenger cruises. The Cunard Line joined the leading passenger cruise line *Carnival Corporation* in 1998.

Cuxhaven > Since 1889 the Hamburg-based Hapag shipping line → **Hapag** had cleared its fast steamships to New York in Cuxhaven in the mouth of Elbe River, which at that time belonged to Hamburg. In return, Hamburg paid for the completion of Cuxhaven's harbor facilities. In 1902, the Hapag Hall overseas train station was completed. To date there are no final figures as to the total number of emigrants who passed through Cuxhaven. Most ships sailing from there were headed for ports in North America. The *Cunard White Star Line* (→ **Cunard Line**) was the first shipping line to resume regular service after World War II in 1948. From September 1948 until March 1950, the two liners *Samaria* and *Scythia* made 27 crossings transporting a total of 26,700 → **Displaced Persons** to Canada. The port of Cuxhaven was unable to compete with the steady growth of → **Air travel** hence discontinuing overseas liner service in 1968.

D

Databases / Family research > Researching ancestors who emigrated to other countries is possible on a number of Internet databases:

Bremen Passenger Records 1920–1939 (Die MAUS)
> www.passagierlisten.de
The archives of the Bremen Chamber of Commerce number 2,953 passenger records of ships departing from the Port of Bremen, 70 percent of which date back to between 1920 and 1939 and refer to ships departing from Bremerhaven for the U.S.A., Canada, South America and Australia. Since July 1999, these passenger lists have been collected and recorded by the Society of Genealogical Research of Bremen in the State Archives of Bremen. The passenger records for ships departing from the Port of Bremen were, with very few exceptions, all

Ellis Island Immigration Museum

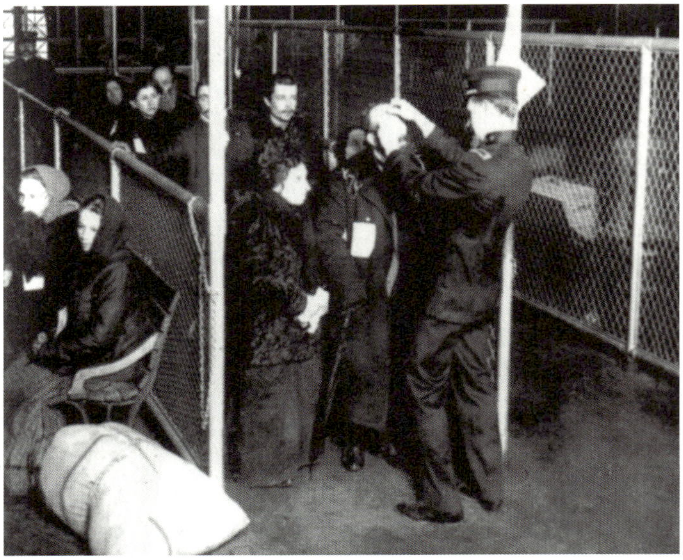

Ellis Island Immigration Museum

Links: Ellis Island und Manhattan, um 1931. Rechts: Ärztliche Untersuchung in der Registry Hall. Anfang des 20. Jahrhunderts führte der U.S. Public Health Service eine Augenuntersuchung ein, der sich jeder Einwanderer in Ellis Island unterziehen musste. / Left: Ellis Island and Manhattan, about 1931. Right: Medical examination in the Registry Hall. The U.S. Public Health Service introduced an eye exam in the early twentieth century which was mandatory for every immigrant arriving at Ellis Island.

destroyed. The passenger records from 1945 on are still subject to data protection.
This data source is accessible online.

Ancestry
> www.ancestry.com
The U.S. database Ancestry works together with the National Archives in Washington, D.C. where the passenger records for ships landing in U.S. ports from all over the world are filed, among them the passenger lists for ships sailing from Hamburg. In addition, the National Archives also keep a record of the U.S. federal censuses which have been carried out every 10 years since 1790. In addition it contains selected German emigration records, German telephone and address directories and the Bremen records of muster rolls and registers of seamen. Ancestry processes the passenger (through 1957) and census records electronically. The data is scanned and made available online. Ancestry.com also features other data on its web site, e.g. military records, birth, marriage & death records and U.S. phone directories.
A fee is charged for using ancestry's online material.

Castle Garden
> www.castlegarden.org
Castle Garden, the first official receiving station in the United States from 1850 until 1890 was the predecessor to Ellis Island. Its database features over 10 million entries for immigrant applications for the period from 1830 till 1892.
Online use of the web site is free of charge.

Ellis Island Passenger Records
> www.ellisisland.org
The *American Family Immigration History Center* was founded in 2001 as part of the *Statue of Liberty—Ellis Island Foundation, Inc.* In 25 million data records available at this research center on Ellis Island visitors can trace ancestors who immigrated to the U.S. between 1892 and 1924 and entered the country through New York.
After setting up a personal password, users have free online access to the database.

Sammlung Deutsches Auswandererhaus / Collection German Emigration Center

Das historische Auswandererhaus wurde bereits wenige Jahre nach seiner Eröffnung 1865 aufgrund zu weniger Übernachtungsgäste wieder geschlossen. Heute ist ein Teil der ehemaligen „Karlsburg" in den Neubau der Hochschule Bremerhaven integriert. / The historic Emigrants' Hostel was closed in 1865, just years after it opened, because of too few overnight guests. Today, structural remnants of the former Karlsburg have been integrated in the new College of Bremerhaven building.

Deportation > Not every emigrant passenger who arrived in the New World was actually allowed to enter the country. The countries of immigration laid down specific immigration requirements which those seeking immigration were required to fulfil. The most common reasons for refusal and hence deportation were certain diseases, physical or mental disabilities, lack of sponsors in the country of immigration or a criminal record. Shipping companies were obligated to pay for the passenger's return ticket to his or her country of origin. Children over the age of 10 had to travel alone in the event the rest of the family had been allowed entrance. The percentage of entrance refusals was, fortunately, low and accounted for only two percent in New York.

Displaced Persons (DPs) > This term is also used in Germany and refers to the approximately seven million persons the western Allied forces encountered in their zones of occupation in May 1945. Either displaced or deported to Germany from all over Europe between 1933 and 1945, the DPs neither wished for nor were able to return to their homes once the war was over. Survivors of concentration camps and labor camps, prisoners of war and laborers from East European countries were initially placed in DP camps in various areas of Germany. Former concentration camps were frequently used for this purpose which caused DPs great suffering as they were reminded daily of the horrors of the Holocaust in addition to the close living quarters and uncertainty as to their future. Hundreds of thousands emigrated to Great Britain, the U.S.A. and Canada. From Bremerhaven alone over 800,000 Displaced Persons set out for new lives in new countries.

E

Ellis Island > The largest receiving station in the U.S. With the influx of immigrants particularly from Eastern Europe as of 1880, **→ Castle Garden** on the southern tip of Manhattan soon became too small. The receiving station at Ellis Island, a small island off Manhattan, was opened in 1892. The large passenger steamships bringing in European immigrants first docked at Hoboken in Manhattan where first- and second-class passengers were allowed to disembark as they had already undergone immigration formalities on board. The steerage passengers, however, disembarked at Ellis Island where they underwent a medical examination and were processed by immigration inspectors before receiving permission to enter the U.S. More than 16 million arrivals registered on Ellis Island by 1954, it had become the largest receiving station in the United States. An estimated two to three percent were refused entrance to the country. Stories of those who were deported (**→ Deportation)** back to their native countries soon gave Ellis Island the name *Island of Tears.*

Sammlung Deutsches Auswandererhaus / Collection German Emigration Center

Auslaufender Dampfer mit Auswanderern, vermutlich in einem englischen Hafen, um 1880. Gemälde von Charlie W. Wyllie. / Steamship with emigrants on board sailing out of an harbor, possibly in England, about 1880. Painting by Charlie W. Wyllie.

Emigrants > People who intend to settle in a foreign country on a permanent basis.

Emigration agents > So-called emigration agents were hired by shipping lines and ship brokers to recruit willing emigrants throughout Europe.

Emigration Center > This set-up, unique in the world, was established by the Bremen merchant Johann George Claussen in Bremerhaven in 1850 and offered up to 2,000 travelers affordable room and board and better sanitary facilities than the taverns and honkytonks in the harbor area.

Emigration waves (mass emigration) > Migration statistics are frequently portrayed as line charts and the upward trends referred to as waves. In researching the reasons causing peak migratory movement there is often evidence of a delayed reaction to economic crises, with emigration commonly setting in about five to ten years later. Crop failure and ensuing famine were additional reasons for the onset of emigration in the nineteenth century. Ireland was hardest-hit by this occurrence. Several potato crops failed in short succession between 1846 and 1851; close to one million people died of starvation, a further million emigrated to the United States. See also **→ Chain Migration**

Entry and residence regulations for Argentina > The government-aided program for European emigration to Argentina, beginning during the first half of the 18th century and stipulated in Article 20 of the Constitution of 1853. "Mass emigration," however, did not take place until 1870 when the country had become politically stable. The increase in socialistic anarchistic

labor strikes beginning in 1890 led to the Law of Residency (*ley de residencia*) which entitled the authorities to expel immigrants or refuse their entry to the country if they were considered a threat to public order. Despite these negative developments, blamed entirely on immigrant laborers, the government-aided immigration program continued to be significant.

It wasn't until 1930 and the military coup against President Hipólito Yrigoyen that the liberal era and, largely with it, the unrestricted immigration policy ended. A new law went into effect on 1 January 1933 restricting immigration to family unification (*llamadas familiares*) and colonists in agricultural settlements. As a result of the Évian Conference the *Circular 11* was signed in Argentina on 12 July 1938, a secret directive designed to stop the immigration of "undesired persons" (Jewish refugees, in particular) to Argentina.

Exile > In contrast to the term "emigration" migration researchers define the term "exile" as a form of extraterritorial migration with the objective of returning to the native country. Hence the U.S.A. is a country of emigration and not of exile as no legal provision has been made for the temporary acceptance of people seeking political or religious asylum.

Expulsion / Expelled > Expulsion is the forced emigration of individuals or entire ethnic groups from areas populated by them. After the war, ethnic Germans were expelled from historically Eastern German areas in present-day Poland, the Czech Republic, Slovakia, Hungary, Yugoslavia, the German province of Eastern Prussia, the later Kaliningrad Oblast of Russia, Lithuania, and other East European countries. The decision for a population transfer of German minorities to the Allied occupation zones in post-war Germany to avoid cultural and ethnic conflicts and violence in the future was made before the war was over. See also **→ Aussiedler / Spätaussiedler**

Historisches Archiv der Hapag-Lloyd AG

Hermann Heinrich Meier (1809–1898), Mitbegründer des „Norddeutschen Lloyd". Gemälde von Wilhelm Bellstedt, o. J. / Hermann Heinrich Meier (1809–1898), founder of the *North German Lloyd* shipping line. Painting by Wilhelm Bellstedt, date unknown.

F

Farewell > "Goodbye," perhaps forever, or at least for quite a long time.

Fugitives > In contrast to refugees, a fugitive is a person fleeing justice. (Former) German Nazis who fall into this category are Adolf Eichmann, Josef Mengele and Erich Priebke.

G

Genealogy > The study of ancestry and lineage. One speaks of family research when research exceeds the purely biological background of mankind.

Geneva Convention > The purpose of the *Geneva Convention*, adopted at a U.N. special conference in July 1951, is to create a uniform legal status for all **→ refugees** who are not awarded diplomatic protection in their native country. All 146 member states are committed to granting **→ asylum** to refugees. The *Geneva Convention* and its 1967 Protocol are the legal foundation for the *United Nations High Commissioner for Refugees* (UNHCR).

German Emigration Center Foundation > The German Emigration Center in Bremerhaven is a public-private partnership project built with public funds and under private management since its opening in August 2005. The *German Emigration Center Foundation* was formed in January 2006 with the aim of promoting large, cost-intensive projects and in the interest of promoting the museum´s aims on an international scale. The *German Emigration Center Foundation* is also a public-private partnership project, formed by the joint efforts of the *Initiativkreis Deutsches Auswandererhaus e.V.* (German Emigration Center Initiative), representatives of the Bremerhaven business community, the city of Bremerhaven and the German Emigration Center´s operating company.

The purpose of this foundation is to enable the German Emigration Center in Bremerhaven to carry out profound research on the history of emigration, thereby focusing specifically on the historic and current significance of emigration for Germany, Europe, the United States of America, and other receiving countries, and to arrange special events, exhibitions, projects and publications, and to make these accessible to a broad public in Germany as well as abroad. Further, the foundation´s tasks include, for example, acquiring exhibits and collections related to emigration, expanding and updating research data in the database and the archives, endorsing conferences and exhibitions dedicated to the scientific study of migration during the nineteenth and twentieth centuries as well as current migratory movements and ensuring that these are addressed to the general public. Furthermore, the foundation sees it as its task to promote student exchange among the countries of Europe and overseas and to award research grants.

> www.stiftung-dah.org

Globalization > Increasing global networking of individuals and business affects economic relations (e.g. company mergers) as well as personal social relations (e.g. Internet). Critics of globalization argue that jobs are being transferred to countries with lower wage levels and that, consequently, major companies based in wealthy countries profit while countries with lesser economic power lose out. Advocates of globaliza-

Historisches Archiv der Hapag-Lloyd AG

Wartehalle des „Norddeutschen Lloyd" an der Kaiserschleuse in Bremerhaven, Anfang der 1920er Jahre. / The *North German Lloyd* Waiting Hall at the Kaiserschleuse in Bremerhaven in the early 1920s.

tion maintain that greater economic and social union on multiple levels may result from the coalescence of markets and businesses.

H

Hapag / Hapag-Lloyd > Triggered by the rapidly growing importance of Bremerhaven as a port of emigration, the *Hamburg-Amerikanische Packetfahrt-Actien-Gesellschaft* (Hapag) was formed in 1847 with the aim of participating in the business of emigration by setting up a direct sailing ship route from Hamburg to North America. Whereas → **North German Lloyd** (NGL) started out with steamship service, it wasn't until 1889 that the Hapag put steamships into service. The shipping line also sold holiday cruises. Hapag opened an emigration village providing accommodation for up to 5,000 in 1901 (see also → **Veddel**). Hapag and NGL lost their entire fleets as reparation to the Allied forces after both world wars. The two shipping companies cooperated in rebuilding their fleets and passenger service after 1954 to avoid competition. Hapag merged with NGL in 1970 to become *Hapag-Lloyd AG*. Major Hapag ships include the *Augusta Victoria* (1889) and the *Fuerst Bismarck* (1891), the fastest ship sailing on the North American route at the time. On her maiden voyage out the *Deutschland* won the → **Blue Ribbon** in 1900, and the *Imperator* (1913) and *Vaterland* (1914) were both the largest ships of their time.

Home / Homeland > For many people, the term home, homeland or native country is but a mere geographical location to which they feel close, where they feel at home. Thus, home is the direct opposite of anything foreign or a life in exile. Home is often but not always the place where a person was born (adopted country). The German word *Heimat*—home or homeland—has its roots in romanticism and is a subject of controversy in Germany because of its ethnic and national overtones.

Hyphen-Americans > Numerous ethnic groups living in the U.S.A. still feel deeply connected to their native country despite the fact that they are American citizens, and maintain cultural habits, traditions and customs. Italian-Americans, African-Americans, Polish-Americans and other hyphen-Americans are very loyal U.S. citizens, define their citizenship primarily politically and consider themselves members of the American immigrant society.

I

IMIS—Institute for Migration Research and Intercultural Studies > The Institute for Migration Research and Intercultural Studies is an interdisciplinary and interdepartmental research institute at the University of Osnabrück in Germany focusing on historic and present-day migratory movement as well as the political, social and cultural aspects of migration and integration.
> www.imis.uni-osnabrueck.de

Integration → Acculturation / Assimilation

M

Meier, Hermann Heinrich > The Bremen businessman and politician (1809–1898) founded the → **North German Lloyd** shipping line in 1857 which soon developed into one of the world's largest shipping lines.

Melting pot / Salad bowl > The U.S.A. was long referred to by sociologists as a melting pot in which immigrants with diverse ethnic backgrounds mixed to create a culture all their own. This perception has been increasingly revised and replaced by the multicultural concept of the salad

Sammlung Deutsches Auswandererhaus / Collection German Emigration Center

Die „Cap Polonio" an den Landungsbrücken im Hamburg, um 1930. / The *Cap Polonio* docked at the Landungsbrücken in Hamburg, about 1930.

bowl, a non-homogeneous yet in itself structured and harmonious unit.

Migrant workers > This term refers to people who immigrate to a certain country for a certain length of time to work. This type of immigration has always had economic reasons.
During the so-called "Economic Miracle" in West Germany in the 1950s there was a shortage of labor. From the late 1950s until 1973, the year when manpower recruitment outside Germany was stopped, an estimated 14 million migrant workers came to Germany from Turkey, Italy and Spain, of which eleven million returned to their home countries while the rest remained in Germany, brought their families to the country, settling there permanently. Albeit to a far lesser degree, foreign laborers were also recruited by the German Democratic Republic, principally from Vietnam.

Migration > The migratory movement of individuals or groups of people connected with a short- or long-term, or permanent change of residence. Migration refers to both emigration and immigration. Domestic migration refers to a change of residence within the same country whereas transit migration means leaving one country to take up residence in another.
The reasons for emigrating and the degree to which this decision is voluntary vary greatly and one distinguishes between **→ Emigrants**, **→ Displaced Persons**, **→ Migrant workers**, and **→ Refugee**.

Missler Halls > In order to solve the accommodation problem for emigrants in transit in Bremen awaiting departure from Bremerhaven the *North German Lloyd* shipping line, together with its main agent Friedrich Missler, built emigration halls in Bremen-Findorff in 1906 / 1907. The halls were designed to offer emigrants from Eastern and Southeastern Europe particularly adequate room and board at a very low price. This type of set-up had already proved highly successful in Hamburg-Veddel. The so-called *Missler Halls*—new accommodations with a capacity of over 2,700 persons—were completed in 1907. After Missler's death, **→ North German Lloyd** took over the building, renaming it *Lloydheim*, and using it to accommodate its passengers.

N

New Immigrants > Towards the turn of the century an increasing number of South and East Europeans immigrated to America, in particular Italians and Greeks as well as Catholics and Jews from East Europe. These immigrants outnumbered so-called old immigrants from northern and northwestern European countries for the first time in 1896. Many Americans watched this development with unease as the new immigrants were regarded a threat to American society and hence marginalized. A heated discussion on immigration restrictions ensued, culminating ultimately in the **→ Quota Act** of 1921, a law regulating immigration on the basis of a quota system, which was definitely to the disadvantage of East and Southeast European immigrants.

North German Lloyd (NGL) > The *Norddeutscher Lloyd* or *North German Lloyd*—steamship shipping line, formed in Bremen in 1857, was the first shipping company to offer regular service between Germany and New York. During the German Empire (1871–1918), NGL grew into one of the largest shipping companies in the world with routes to the U.S.A., South America and Australia. Whereas the majority of passengers were emigrants, NGL made millions on American and German tourist passages as well. The company's home port was Bremerhaven where, in 1869, NGL opened the first port waiting hall at *Neuer Hafen* followed by a second one at Kaiserschleuse in 1897. With ships constantly increasing in size, the Bremerhaven port and lock facilities had become too small so that NGL ships sailed from Nordenham, on the West banks of the Weser River across from Bremerhaven, between 1890 and 1896. From the outset NGL operated its own docks in Bremerhaven for ship maintenance and repair work. This repair yard ultimately became known as *Lloyd Werft Bremerhaven*, still in existence today and one of the foremost shipyards for ship conversion and lengthening. Among the most prominent NGL-owned ships were the four-stacked steamship *Kaiser Wilhelm der Grosse*, the *Columbus*, the *Europa* and the *Bremen*, the latter winning the **→ Blue Ribbon** for the fastest transatlantic crossing in 1929. In 1970, the two top shipping competitors, NGL and Hapag, merged to form **→ Hapag-Lloyd**.

P

Pilgrim fathers > Persecuted in England for religious separatism the Puritan pilgrim fathers emigrated to America in the seventeenth century and became the first English settlers in New England. The story of the *Mayflower* is legendary: in 1602 the ship set sail for America with 102 passengers—predominantly pilgrims—on board. The ship left Plymouth, England on September 16, arriving in Plymouth, Massachusetts on November 11.

Pogrom > The term *pogrom* (Russian for devastation, destruction, riot) means riots against religious, national or ethnic minorities and has come to stand for violence and looting closely related to anti-Jewish sentiment. In czarist Russia repeated pogroms between 1881 and 1913 led to mass emigration of Russian Jews to the United States and Palestine. In Nazi Germany the anti-Jewish pogroms of November 1938 were government-initiated. The last big pogrom directed against the Jews to take place in Europe was in Kielce, Poland in 1946.

Ports of emigration > The major ports of emigration for German emigrants up through the mid-nineteenth century were Rotterdam, Holland; Antwerp, Belgium; Le Havre, France; and Liverpool and Southampton in England. Emigrants from countries in Southern or Southeastern Europe customarily departed from Genoa, Italy. As a result of the → **Bremen Decree** and the building of an → **Emigration Center** as well as the internationally successful shipping line → **North German Lloyd**, Bremerhaven began to develop into Germany's most important port of emigration as of the mid-nineteenth century. Bremerhaven was the home port for the *North German Lloyd* shipping line although its ships sailed under the flag of Bremen, as Bremerhaven is part of the city-state of Bremen. A total of 7.2 million people departed for the New World by way of Bremerhaven between 1830 and 1974. Shiploads of emigrants departed from Hamburg on board sailing ships and later steamships, but this was to change by the end of the nineteenth century. Whereas the passenger steamship company → **Hapag** was located in Hamburg, Hapag ships invariably sailed from Cuxhaven as of 1889 for the simple reason that the latter was more easily accessible. More than five million passengers sailed for the New World on board ships flying the flag of Hamburg.

Ports of immigration > There were a number of major ports of immigration in the New World, with the East Coast of the U.S. ranking among those most preferred by European immigrants. While New York was the leading U.S. port of immigration, two million entered through Baltimore, the second-largest port of immigration, and one million through Philadelphia. Other favored destinations were Boston, and New Orleans and Galveston in the South, particularly for immigrants heading for Texas. In contrast to New Orleans, the port of Galveston was sufficiently deep to accept larger ships, thus rendering New Orleans irrelevant after 1855. By 1900 over 100,000 immigrants had entered the U.S. through Galveston, of which the majority were Germans who had sailed from Bremerhaven. South America attracted numerous immigrants as well, with 6.6 million Europeans immigrating to Argentina between 1850 and 1940, mostly through Buenos Aires. Brazil was also high on the list of preferred countries with people from more than 50 nations immigrating through Rio de Janeiro and Santos between 1819 and 1974, among them Italians, Portuguese, Spanish and Germans. The port of Montevideo in Uruguay, opened in 1868, was South America's most advanced port of transshipment. Immigrants to Canada commonly arrived in the ports of Quebec or Halifax, the latter evolving into Canada's largest port. An estimated six millions persons entered Canada through these two ports. Australia has also always figured among the major countries of immigration since the beginning of mass migration with several million immigrants entering the fifth continent through the ports of Melbourne and Sydney.

Q

Quota Act > The *Emergency Quota Act* of May 19, 1921 greatly restricted annual immigration levels to the U.S., limiting it to three percent of every nationality living in the U.S. since 1910 and clearly favoring immigrants from Northern and Western Europe. Census data recorded the total number of immigrants at 357,802, of which more than half were from countries in Northern and Western Europe. The *Quota Act* meant a 75-percent reduction in immigrants from Southern and Eastern Europe as compared to previous years. The quota system based on countries of origin reflects the fear of foreigners that had been rising steadily for decades. The U.S.A. tightened its immigration policy still further with the *National Origins Act* in 1924, limiting immigration to an annual 164,000 and a maximum two percent from every nationality residing in the U.S. since 1890.

R

Raphaels-Werk > This Christian agency, established in 1871 and named after the archangel Raphael, known to protect travelers, has always provided advice and consultation for migrants leaving Germany temporarily or permanently. The church-affiliated *Evangelische Auswandererberatung e.V.* (Protestant Service for Migration Advice), recently renamed Overseas Advice, was an agency offering advice and consultation to migrants.
\> www.raphaels-werk.de
\> www.ev-auslandsberatung.de

Ratline > A term coined by U.S. intelligence officers describing systems of escape routes for Nazis and other fascists fleeing Europe after World War II. The route went from Germany to Italy, Southern Italy or Rome, to South America—and, in particular, Argentina. Countless Nazi escaped justice for crimes committed during the National Socialist dictatorship in Germany (1933–1945).

Refugee > In contrast to emigrants, refugees are forced to leave their country for a certain period of time or permanently due to persecution or the threat of persecution. In accordance with the 1951 → **Geneva Convention** refugees are persons, who due to the very real threat of persecution, seek refuge outside their native country or who seek refuge as a stateless person outside their usual country of residence. Reasons of persecution recognized by the *Geneva Convention* are race, religion, nationality, affiliation with a certain social group and political conviction.

S

Ship classes > The technical development of ships altered the conditions for transatlantic and other ocean crossings immensely, particularly for steerage-class passengers. Whereas hundreds of emigrants were cramped in the between-deck bunks and suffered catastrophic sanitary conditions for a period of as many as 18 weeks, with many dying en route, sailing time to America dropped to eight to 15 days on board the fast steamers, which also provided adequate sanitary facilities for steerage passengers. Larger ship engines and improved drive technology on board → **North German Lloyd** liners as of 1897 shortened the transatlantic crossing to a mere six days. From 1906, NGL steamers were even equipped with a dining hall for steerage passengers. By the end of the 1920s, shared cabins replaced mass accommodations on board and a tourist class had been introduced.

Society of Friends of the German Emigration Center (Freundeskreis Deutsches Auswandererhaus e.V.) > Society of Friends, established in 2005, originated in the *German Emigration Center Development Association*, founded in 1985. While the Development Association spent 20 years promoting the construction of the Emigration Center in Bremerhaven, Society of Friends focuses on developing and adding on to the program of events offered by the museum since its opening in August 2005 featuring talks and informative events centering on the topic of migration, particularly Bremerhaven and Bremen as ports of emigration. The Society of Friends library, covering over 2,000 volumes on migration, has been given to the German Emigration Center on permanent loan.

T

Transit migration > In the late 1900s and during the Weimar Republic large numbers of emigrants from Southern and Eastern Europe traversed the German Empire on their way to Hamburg and Bremerhaven from where they sailed for the New World.

V

Veddel > In order to reroute the steadily growing stream of emigrants past the center of Hamburg, in 1898 the Hamburg-based shipping line→ **Hapag** built so-called emigration halls on the Elbe island of Veddel, which separates the North Elbe and the South Elbe Rivers. Opened in 1901, this accommodation was constantly enlarged, finally totaling a full 55,000 square meters and about 30 individual buildings. The decentralized location and, for that time, unusually good sanitary facilities, were a direct result of the cholera epidemic which had broken out in 1892 and was attributed to Russian emigrants. Upon arrival at Veddel, each immigrant was subjected to a medical examination, and possibly placed in quarantine for 14 days. At the same time, impecunious immigrants were kept at a distance from the center of town.
In addition to dormitories and social facilities the complex included a large dining hall, bathrooms and a disinfecting station. There were a Catholic and Protestant church as well as a Jewish synagogue. Following enlargement in 1906/1907 meals for Jewish and Christian emigrants were prepared in separate kitchens and served in separate dining halls. The emigration halls served as field hospitals during World War I. Reopened for their original purpose the emigration halls were seized by the SS in 1934. Until then, primarily Jewish refugees had departed for America via Hamburg.
Used later as warehouses, the halls were eventually torn down. An emigration museum by the name of *BallinStadt* opened here in July 2007.

Visa > An official permit authorizing a person to pass the border into the country issuing the visa. A visa was and is required for immigration and is a primary element of the migration process.

Volga Germans > This collective term refers to ethnic Germans who lived along the River Volga and the Black Sea. In 1762/1763, Catherine the Great, Empress of Russia, invited Germans and other Europeans to immigrate to Russia and develop the land. By 1864, more than three hundred colonies had been founded. A main reason for their immigration had been special rights granted them for preserving cultural (and linguistic) independence. When, in 1871, these were revoked to a great extent by reforms instituted by Czar Alexander II, a large number decided to emigrate to North and South America.

W

White Star Line > The *Aberdeen White Star Line* was formed in 1845 during the course of the Australian Gold Rush for the purpose of transporting gold and other goods from Australia back to Europe. Its real breakthrough came when it switched from sailing ships to steamships for transatlantic routes. Several ships won the → **Blue Ribbon** (among them the *Adriatic*, 1872; the *Germanic*, 1875, the *Teutonic* and the *Majestic*, both 1891) until a later owner decided to emphasize size and luxury instead of speed. After the loss of its two most prominent vessels, the *Titanic* and its sister ship, the *Britannic*, the *White Star Line* was on the verge of bankruptcy. It merged with the → **Cunard Line** to form the *Cunard White Star Line*.

Y

Yerba > The main ingredient in mate tea, the national drink of Argentina. The word mate is rooted in the indigenous term for the hollowed-out gourd used as a drinking vessel. However, the Spanish word yerba actually refers to the tea plant itself.

Z

Zech, Paul (1881–1946) > One of the most diverse and prolific German writers of the early 20th century. As a sympathizer of the German *Social Democratic Party* (SPD) Zech attracted the attention of the Nazi regime in 1933. Following a short period of imprisonment he left Germany. His escape took him to exile in Argentina where he died in 1946. The works he wrote during his years in South America (1933–1946) are classified as German exile literature.

LANDKARTEN, DATEN, FAKTEN / MAPS, FACTS AND FIGURES

117

LANDKARTEN, DATEN, FAKTEN zur Migration

MAPS, FACTS AND FIGURES on Migration

Aus- und Einwanderung, Flucht und Vertreibung sind weltweite, permanente Prozesse. Deutschland ist nunmehr seit knapp 200 Jahren entweder Aus- oder Einwanderungsland, manchmal sogar beides gleichzeitig, wie es zurzeit der Fall ist. Diagramme zeigen in Zahlen die unterschiedlichsten Aspekte von 200 Jahren Migration von und nach Deutschland.

Emigration and immigration, expulsion and refuge are worldwide, permanent processes. Germany has been a country of migration, i.e. migratory in- and outflow, for close to 200 years. At times, migratory in- and outflow occurred simultaneously, as is presently the case. The figures in the diagrams illustrate the various aspects of 200 years of migration to and from Germany.

1 | Herkunftsstaaten der größten ausländischen Gruppen in Deutschland
Major Groups of Foreign Nationals in Germany and Their Countries of Origin

Ende 2008 leben knapp 6,73 Millionen Personen in Deutschland, die ausschließlich eine ausländische Staatsangehörigkeit besitzen; das sind knapp 8,2 Prozent der Gesamtbevölkerung. Die Türken stellen mit rund 1.688.000 Personen die größte Ausländergruppe in Deutschland, zu ihnen gehören 2,0 Prozent der Gesamtbevölkerung. / By late 2008, just under 6.73 million foreign nationals were living in Germany, i.e. roughly 8.2 percent of the total population. With a total of 1,688,000, the Turks represent the largest group of foreign nationals, that is 2.0 percent of the total population.

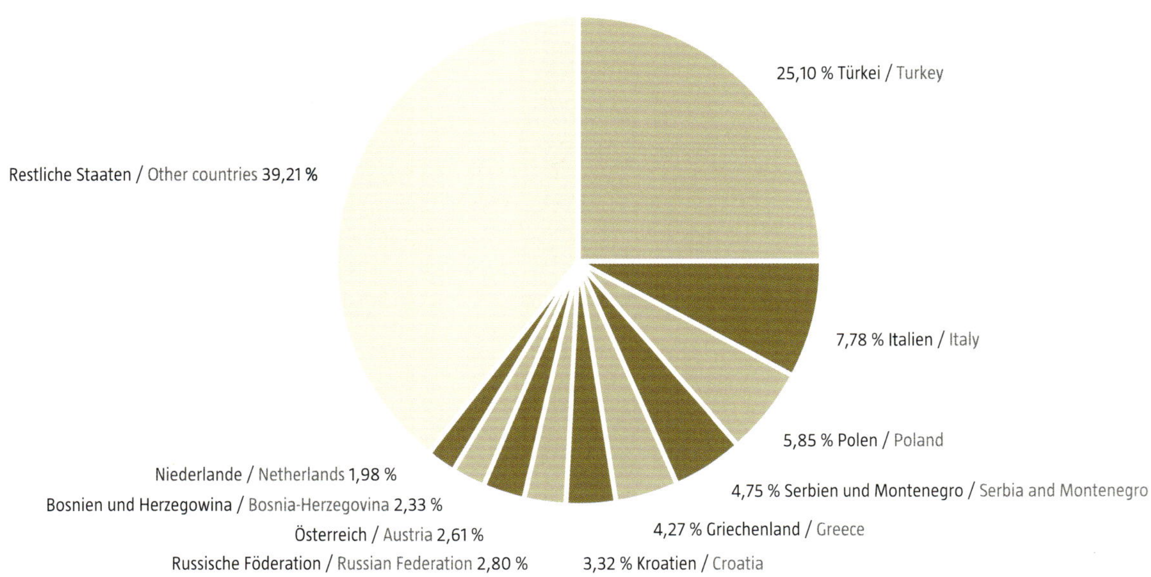

Quelle: / Source: Statistisches Bundesamt, Wiesbaden, Stand 31.12.2008.

2 | Wanderungen von Deutschen und Ausländern über die Grenzen Deutschlands 1954–2007
Migration of German and Foreign Nationals Beyond German Borders 1954–2007

Deutschland ist in Bewegung: Jedes Jahr wandern Hunderttausende in das Land ein oder aus. Durch die zurückgehende Zahl von Zuzügen und die zunehmende Zahl von Fortzügen von Deutschen ergibt sich für den Zeitraum 2005 bis 2007 erstmals seit Ende der 1960er Jahre ein Wanderungsverlust. Bei Ausländern ist weiterhin ein Wanderungsgewinn zu verzeichnen. / Germany is on the move. Every year, hundreds of thousands emigrate from or immigrate to Germany. The declining inflow of immigrants and increasing outflow of German nationals between 2005 and 2007 resulted for the first time since the 1960s in an overall migration loss. Net immigration of foreign nationals continues to be registered.

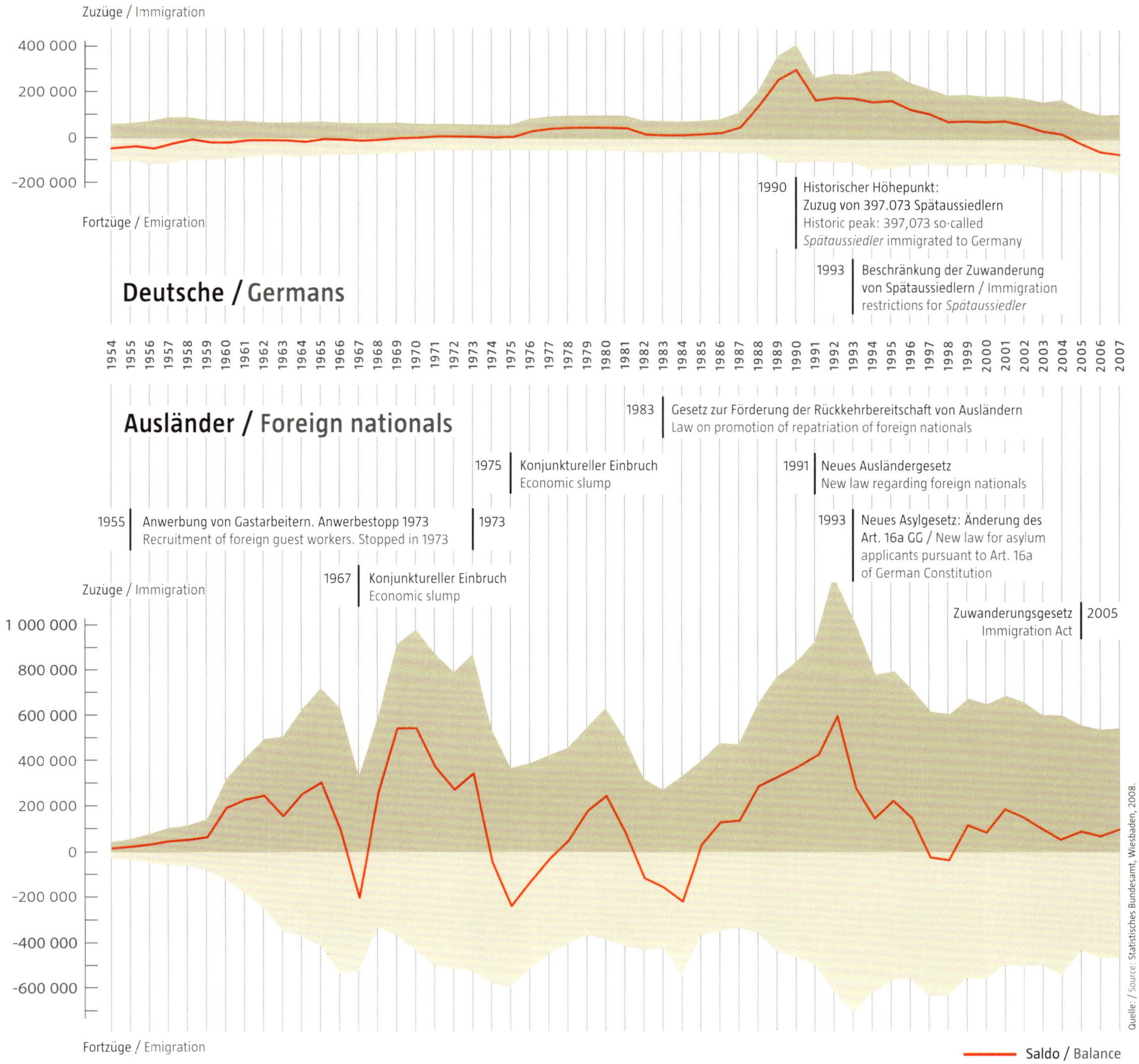

Bis 1990 früheres Bundesgebiet. Ab 1991 mit den neuen Bundesländern.

Earlier federal territory up to 1990. As of 1991, including the newly formed German States.

3 | Spätaussiedler nach Herkunftsländern 1985–2008
Spätaussiedler (German Resettlers) and their Countries of Origin 1985–2008

Die Spätaussiedler, die gemäß Artikel 116 des Grundgesetzes Deutsche sind, bilden vor den Türken, Italienern, Polen und Griechen die größte Gruppe von Einwanderern in Deutschland. Zwischen 1991 und 2008 wanderten 3.240.099 Spätaussiedler nach Deutschland ein. Bedingt durch verschärfte Einwanderungskriterien, insbesondere durch das 2005 in Kraft getretene Zuwanderungsgesetz und die gesunkene Zahl der Auswanderungswilligen in den Herkunftsländern, ist die Zahl stark rückläufig. / The *Spätaussiedler* who pursuant to Article 116 of the German Constitution are ethnic Germans, account for the largest group of German immigrants, well ahead of the Turks, Italians, Polish and Greeks. Between 1991 and 2008 alone, a total of 3,240,099 *Spätaussiedler* immigrated to Germany. Tighter immigration criteria, due particularly to the Immigration Act effective as of 2005 and the reduced number of people in the countries of origin willing to resettle in Germany, have caused the number to drop significantly.

	Ehemalige Sowjetunion [1] Former Soviet Union [1]	Polen Poland	Rumänien Romania	Ehemalige Tschechoslowakei [2] Former CSFR [2]	Ungarn Hungary	Ehemaliges Jugoslawien [3] Former Yugoslavia [3]	Sonstige Länder Other countries	**Gesamt Total**
1985	460	22 075	14 924	757	485	191	76	**38 968**
1986	753	27 188	13 130	882	584	182	69	**42 788**
1987	14 488	48 423	13 994	835	581	156	46	**78 523**
1988	47 572	140 226	12 902	949	763	223	38	**202 673**
1989	98 134	250 340	23 387	2 027	1 618	1 469	80	**377 055**
1990	147 950	133 872	111 150	1 708	1 336	961	96	**397 073**
1991	147 320	40 129	32 178	927	952	450	39	**221 995**
1992	195 576	17 742	16 146	460	354	199	88	**230 565**
1993	207 347	5 431	5 811	134	37	120	8	**218 888**
1994	213 214	2 440	6 615	97	40	182	3	**222 591**
1995	209 409	1 677	6 519	62	43	178	10	**217 898**
1996	172 181	1 175	4 284	14	14	77	6	**177 751**
1997	131 895	687	1 777	8	18	34	0	**134 419**
1998	101 550	488	1 005	16	4	14	3	**103 080**
1999	103 599	428	855	11	4	19	0	**104 916**
2000	94 558	484	547	18	2	0	6	**95 615**
2001	97 434	623	380	22	2	17	6	**98 484**
2002	90 587	553	256	13	3	4	0	**91 416**
2003	72 289	444	137	2	5a	8	0	**72 885**
2004	58 728	278	76	3	0	8	0	**59 093**
2005	35 396	80	39	4	3	0	0	**35 522**
2006	7 626	80	40	0	0	0	1	**7 747**
2007	5 695	70	21	0	0	0	6	**5 792**
2008	4 301	44	16	0	0	0	1	**4 362**
	2 258 062	**694 977**	**266 189**	**8 949**	**6 848**	**4 492**	**582**	**3 240 099**

Quelle: / Source: Bundesverwaltungsamt, Köln, 2009.

[1] 1991 Auflösung der UdSSR, Gründung der Gemeinschaft Unabhängiger Staaten (GUS) als Zusammenschluss verschiedener Nachfolgestaaten der ehemaligen Sowjetunion. 1991 Breakup of U.S.S.R., formation of CIS (Commonwealth of Independent States), a federation of several states evolving from former U.S.S.R.

[2] 1948–1990 Tschechoslowakische Sozialistische Republik (ČSSR), 1990–1993 Tschechoslowakische Föderative Republik (ČSFR), 01.01.1993 Auflösung der ČSFR nach einvernehmlicher Trennung. Seitdem Tschechische Republik und Slowakei. / 1948–1990 Czechoslovakian Socialist Republic (Č.S.S.R.), 1990–2003 Czechoslovakian Federal Republic (Č.S.F.R.), as of January 1, 1993 joint agreement to dissolve Č.S.F.R., forming two separate entities, the Czech Republic and Slovakia.

[3] 1963–1992 Sozialistische Föderative Republik Jugoslawien, 1992–2003 Bundesrepublik Jugoslawien, 2003–2006 Serbien und Montenegro. Am 03.06.2006 Unabhängigkeitserklärung der Republik Montenegro. Am 28.06.2006 Aufnahme Montenegros als 192. Mitglied in die UNO. / 1963–1992 Socialistic Federal Republic of Yugoslavia, 1992–2003 Federal Republic of Yugoslavia, 2003–2006 Serbia and Montenegro. Declaration of independence by the Republic of Montenegro on June 3, 2006. On June 28, 2006 Montenegro becomes the 192nd member of the U.N.

4 Eingebürgerte Personen im Jahr 2007
Naturalized Citizens in 2007

Als im Jahr 2000 das neue Staatsangehörigkeitsrecht in Kraft trat, entschieden sich 186.688 Ausländer für die deutsche Staatsbürgerschaft. In den Folgejahren war die Zahl rückläufig. Im Jahr 2006 stieg die Zahl erstmals wieder auf 124.830 Personen, sank im Jahr 2007 jedoch wiederum um knapp 9,5 Prozent auf 113.030. / With the enforcement of the Nationality Act in Germany in 2000, 186,688 foreign nationals chose to acquire German citizenship. That figure dropped in the years thereafter. In 2006, the number rose to 124,830 persons again, however, then dropped almost 9.5 percent to 113,030 in 2007.

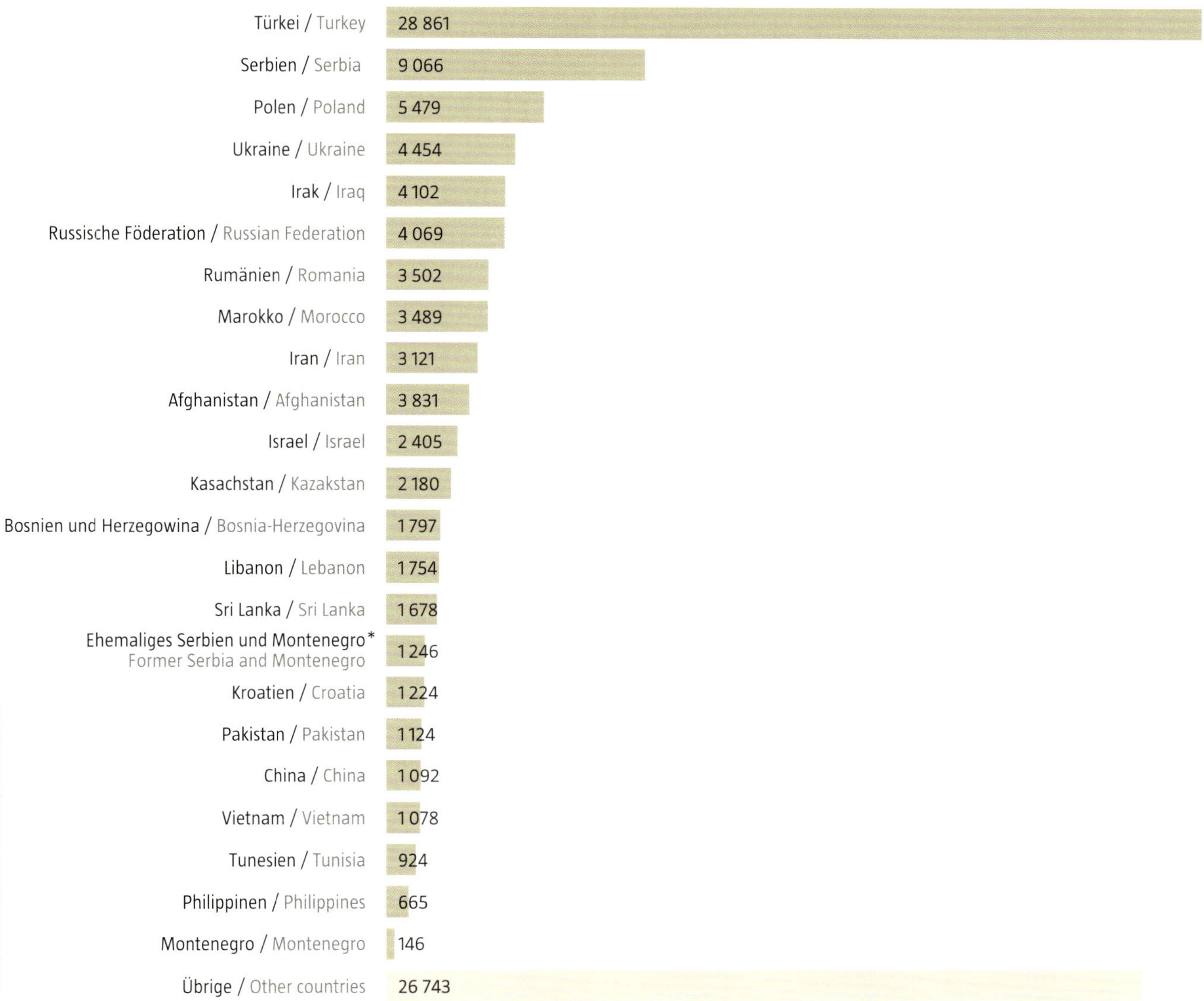

Quelle:/ Source: Statistisches Bundesamt, Wiesbaden, 2008.

* Ab August 2006 werden neben der Staatsangehörigkeit von Serbien und Montenegro auch die Staatsangehörigkeit der beiden Nachfolgestaaten „Serbien" und „Montenegro" nachgewiesen. / After August 2006, in addition to nationals from Serbia and Montenegro nationals from the successor states of "Serbia" and "Montenegro" were also registered.

5 Asylerstanträge in Deutschland 1995, 2000 und 2007
First Applications for Asylum in Germany in 1995, 2000 and 2007

Die Zahl der Asylanträge fällt weiter und erreichte 2007 den niedrigsten Stand seit 1983. Verhandelt wurden im Jahr 2007 insgesamt 19.164 Asylerstanträge; ein weiterer Rückgang um 8,9 Prozent zum Vorjahr. Die Flucht vor Kriegen und Bürgerkriegen ist z.B. kein Asylgrund, so dass eine Ablehnung erfolgt. Weitere Asylsuchende werden aufgrund der so genannten Dublin-II-Verordnung in ein anderes EU-Land überstellt. Lediglich 304 Personen (1,1 Prozent) wurden als asylberechtigt anerkannt. Bei 26,5 Prozent der übrigen Antragsteller bestand Abschiebeschutz oder es lagen Abschiebehindernisse vor. Kinder unter 16 Jahren machen 34,1 Prozent der Antragssteller aus. / The number of first applications for asylum continued to drop and in 2007 reached an all-time low since 1983. Court hearings for a total of 19,164 first applications were heard in 2007, a further drop of 8.9 percent against the previous year. Fleeing wars or civil wars, for example, is not accepted as a reason for asylum and results in refusal. Still other asylum seekers are transferred to other EU countries as a result of the Dublin Regulation. The applications of only 304 persons (1.1 percent) seeking asylum were granted. Twenty-six percent of the remaining applicants were either under protection from deportation or other reasons prevented their deportation. Of all applicants, 34.1 percent were children under the age of sixteen.

1995 gesamt / total 127 937

Herkunftsland / Country of origin	Erstanträge / First applications
BRep. Jugoslawien / Yugoslavia*	26 227
Türkei / Turkey	25 514
Afghanistan / Afghanistan	7 515
Irak / Iraq	6 880
Sri Lanka / Sri Lanka	6 048
Bosnien und Herzegowina / Bosnia-Herzegovina	4 932
Iran / Iran	3 908
Rumänien / Romania	3 522
Armenien / Armenia	3 383
Pakistan / Pakistan	3 116
Sonstige / Other countries	36 892

2000 gesamt / total 78 564

Herkunftsland / Country of origin	Erstanträge / First applications
Irak / Iraq	11 601
BRep. Jugoslawien / Yugoslavia*	11 121
Türkei / Turkey	8 968
Afghanistan / Afghanistan	5 380
Iran / Iran	4 878
Russische Föderation / Russian Federation	2 763
Syrien / Syria	2 641
Vietnam / Vietnam	2 332
Ungeklärt / Undefined	2 151
China / China	2 072
Sonstige / Other countries	24 657

2007 gesamt / total 19 164

Herkunftsland / Country of origin	Erstanträge / First applications
Irak / Iraq	4 327
Serbien / Serbia*	1 996
Türkei / Turkey	1 437
Vietnam / Vietnam	987
Russische Föderation / Russian Federation	772
Syrien, Arabische Republik / Syria	634
Iran, Iranische Republik / Iran	631
Libanon / Lebanon	592
Nigeria / Nigeria	503
Indien / India	413
Sonstige / Other countries	6 872

* Siehe S. 120, Fußnote 3. / See p. 120, footnote No. 3.

Quelle: / Source: Bundesamt für Migration und Flüchtlinge, Nurnberg, 2008.

6 Deutsche Auswanderung von 1955 bis 2007
German Emigration from 1955 until 2007

Die 15 beliebtesten Zielländer von deutschen Auswanderern im Jahr 2007. Im Jahr 2007 stieg die Zahl der ausgewanderten Deutschen auf 161.105. Als Auswanderer werden in der Bundesrepublik Deutschland diejenigen statistisch erfasst, die ihre alleinige Wohnung oder Hauptwohnung aufgegeben haben. Die Zahlenangaben für den Zeitraum bis 1990 gelten nur für das frühere Bundesgebiet (Westdeutschland). / The top 15 countries among German emigrants in the year 2007. A total of 161,105 Germans emigrated in the year 2007. In the Federal Republic of Germany emigrants are, statistically speaking, those people who have given up their sole or main place of residence in Germany. The figures for the period until 1990 refer to former West Germany.

2007 gesamt / total 161 105

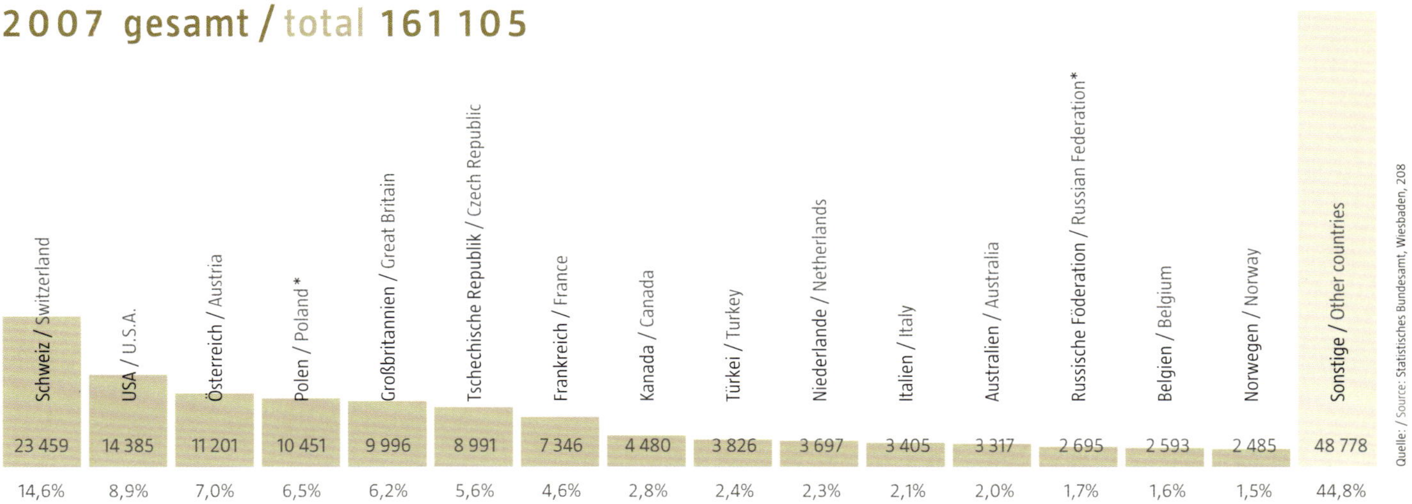

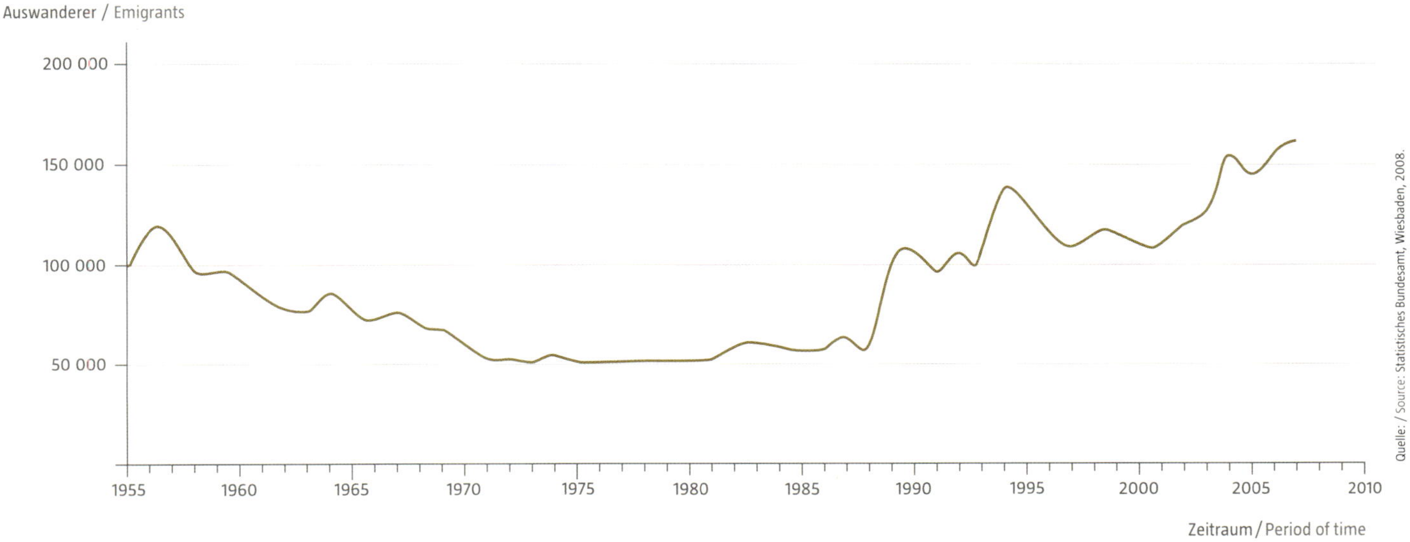

* Viele Spätaussiedler kehren inzwischen wieder nach Polen und in die Russische Föderation zurück. / A large number of emigrants of German origin from Eastern European states (so-called *Spätaussiedler*) have since returned to Poland and the countries of the Russian Federation.

7 Nachfahren der Einwanderer in den USA im Jahr 2000
Descendants of U.S. Immigrants in 2000

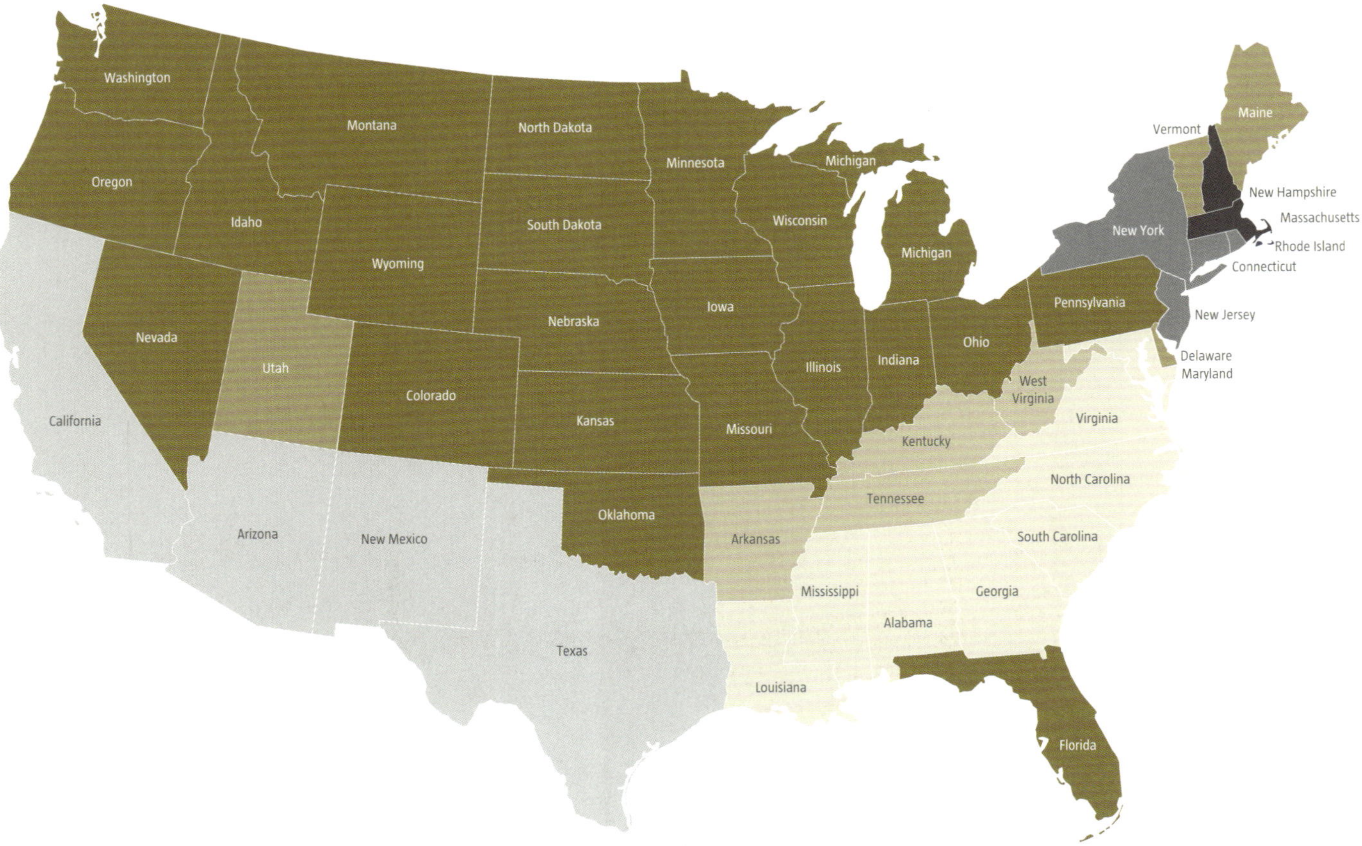

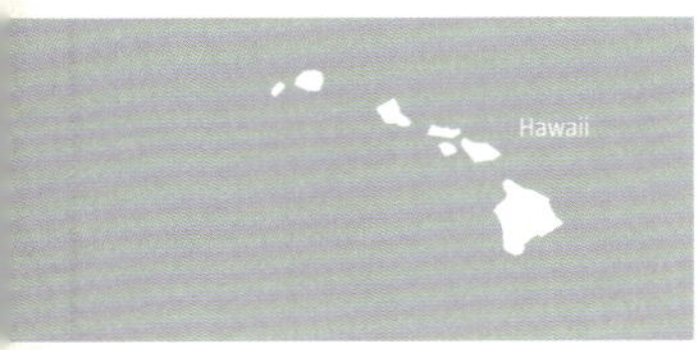

Nach ihren Vorfahren gefragt, sagt der größte Teil der Einwohner des jeweiligen Bundestaates, diese seien:
Asked about their ancestors, the majority of the residents of the respective federal state say their ancestors are:

- Afrikaner / African-American
- Amerikaner / American
- Engländer / English
- Deutsche / German
- Iren / Irish
- Italiener / Italian
- Mexikaner / Mexican
- Sonstige / Other

Sonstige Antworten / Other answers:
Chinesen / Chinese (San Francisco County, California), Kubaner / Cuban (Miami-Dade County, Florida), Dominikaner / Dominican (New York County, New York), Philippiner / Filipino (Kauai and Maui Counties, Hawaii), Frankokanadier / French Canadian (Androskoggin County, Maine), Hawaiianer / Hawaiian (Hawaii State, Honolulu County, Hawaii), Polen / Polish (Luzerne County, Pennsylvania), Portugiesen / Portuguese (Bristol County, MA and Bristol County, Rhode Island)

Quelle: / Source: U.S. Census Bureau, Erhebung 2000, Sondertabellen. / U.S. Census Bureau, Census 2000 special tabulation.

DIE SAMMLUNG / THE COLLECTION

125

DAS HERZ DES MUSEUMS – DIE SAMMLUNG

THE HEART OF THE MUSEUM—THE COLLECTION

KATRIN QUIRIN

In fast jeder deutschen Familie gibt es eine Auswanderin oder einen Auswanderer. Und so finden immer mehr Menschen den Weg ins Deutsche Auswandererhaus, um Fotos, Dokumente und andere Erinnerungsstücke in die Sammlung des Museums zu übergeben.

Elementar ist für uns dabei immer die dazugehörige Geschichte, das Erlebte. Nur durch das Zusammenspiel von Objekt und Ereignis entsteht die emotionale, lebendige Darstellung von Historie. So ist unsere Sammlung ein einzigartiges Zeugnis europäischer Migrationsgeschichte. Heute zählt die Sammlung mehr als 2.800 Objekte – hauptsächlich Fotos, Briefe, persönliche Dokumente, Unterlagen zu Schiffspassagen und Gepäckstücke. Komplettiert wird dies durch die Präsenzbibliothek mit einem Bestand von 5.000 Bänden.

Der Sammlungsschwerpunkt des Deutschen Auswandererhauses liegt in der überseeischen, europäischen Migration über deutsche Häfen (und Flughäfen) 1800 bis heute und dabei im Besonderen in der Auswanderung über Bremerhaven in der Zeit 1830 bis 1974.

There is an emigrant in almost every German family. So it comes as no surprise that an increasing number of people are coming to the German Emigration Center to commit photographs, documents and other memorabilia to the museum's growing collection.

The story behind the object or the experience attached to it is of fundamental importance to us. The interaction of object and event is what brings history to life, infusing it with emotion and meaning. As a result, our collection is a unique testimonial of the history of European migration. At present, the collection numbers more than 2,800 objects—primarily pictures, letters, personal documents, records of passenger lists and baggage supplemented by an extensive reference library of 5,000 volumes.

The German Emigration Center collection focuses on the emigration of Europeans abroad via German ports (and airports) from 1800 through today, most specifically via the Port of Bremerhaven between 1830 and 1974.

BRINGEN SIE UNS IHRE ERINNERUNGSSTÜCKE! / BRING US YOUR MEMORABILIA!

Erzählen Sie uns die Geschichte Ihres ausgewanderten Vorfahrens oder Ihren eigenen Weg in die Neue Welt! Helfen Sie uns, unsere einzigartige Sammlung an Auswanderergeschichten und den dazugehörigen Objekten zu vergrößern! Wir freuen uns auf Ihre Geschichte. / Tell us the story of your ancestors who emigrated or the story of your own journey to the New World! Help us enlarge our unique collection of emigration stories and the objects that go with them. We look forward to hearing your personal account.

Was Auswanderer aufheben und vererben: Erinnerungsstücke / Items Emigrants Kept and Handed Down: Memorabilia

Gepäckstücke / Pieces of Luggage

Im Oktober 1960 reist Christa Franz auf Besuch in die Neue Welt. Ihre ältere Schwester war bereits in den 1950er Jahren in die USA ausgewandert. Mit 500 Dollar (Reise-)Schulden und ohne Englischkenntnisse besteigt sie das Schiff „Bremen" des „Norddeutschen Lloyd" nach New York. Nach zwei Jahren endet ihr Arbeitsaufenthalt und sie entschließt sich, für immer zu bleiben./ Christa Franz traveled to the New World on a visit in October 1960. Her older sister had already emigrated to the United States in the 1950s. Christa boards the *Bremen*, a *North German Lloyd* vessel, for New York without a word of English and five hundred dollars (in travel debt). Her working stay terminates at the end of two years, but she decides to stay for good.

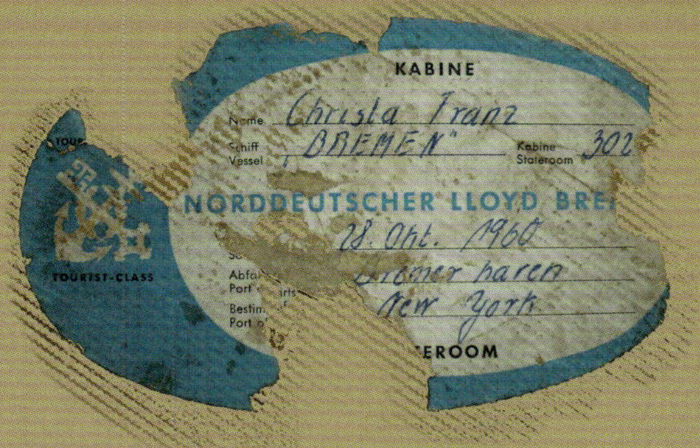

Reisedokumente / Travel Documents

Der deutsche Reisepass von Moses Kirchheimer ist am 30. Juni 1939 in Bremerhaven ausgestellt. Auf der letzten Seite befindet sich das Visum des Amerikanischen Konsulates in Hamburg. Wenige Wochen vor Ausbruch des Zweiten Weltkrieges kann Kirchheimer damit ausreisen.

Das rote große „J" auf der ersten Seite des Passes erzählt von der antijüdischen Gesetzgebung des Nationalsozialismus. Ab Oktober 1938 werden Pässe von deutschen Juden mit diesem Stempel versehen. Er dient dazu, Nichtarier auf den ersten Blick und unübersehbar zu erkennen. Der Pass erzählt die geglückte Flucht eines deutschen Juden aus dem Dritten Reich – jedoch nichts über den Verbleib seiner Familie. Die Nachfahren von Moses Kirchheimer leben heute in New York.

The German passport belonging to Moses Kirchheimer is issued in Bremerhaven on 30 June 1939. A visa from the Consulate of the United States of America in Hamburg is stamped on the last page, allowing him to leave the country just weeks before the Second World War breaks out.

The large red "J" stamped on the first page of his passport reveals the anti-Jewish legislation of the Nazi era. As of October 1938, German Jews are required to have their passports stamped so that they are quickly and easily recognized as non-Aryans. The passport conveys the story of the successful escape of a German Jew during the Third Reich, yet nothing of what happens to the rest of his family. Moses Kirchheimer's descendants live in New York today.

Erinnerungsstücke / Memorabilia

Der Vater der 17-jährigen Martha Hüner meint, dass seine Tochter in Amerika nur einen Cowboy heiraten kann. So gibt er ihr 1923 diese Pferdebürste mit auf den Weg in die USA, die sie ihr Leben lang begleiten soll. Der Cowboy bleibt jedoch aus. Martha heiratet einen deutschen Bäcker. Mit der Bürste wird der Tresen der Bäckerei gesäubert oder sonntags Kuchenkrümel vom Tisch gefegt.

The father of 17-year old Martha Hüner was certain that his daughter would marry a cowboy once she was in America. So, in 1923, he gave her this brush to take with her, a gift that accompanied her her entire life. Martha, however, did not marry a cowboy, but a German baker instead. She used the brush to clean off the bakery counter and to clear the table of crumbs after Sunday dinner.

IMPRESSUM / CREDITS

Impressum Katalog / Credits Catalogue

Herausgeber / Published by
Deutsches Auswandererhaus Bremerhaven
edition DAH

Redaktion / Editorial Staff
Dr. Simone Eick, Kirsten Pörschke, Katrin Quirin

Recherchen, Glossar / Data Research, Glossary
Marina Eismann, Sandra Frey, Karin Heß, Janina Kriszio,
Katrin Quirin, Steffen Wiegmann

Lektorat / Editor
Katrin Quirin

Kataloggestaltung / Graphic Design
Studio Andreas Heller, Hamburg
Daniele Gasparini, Jutta Strauß

Übersetzung / Translator
Julie Penzel-Althoff

Fotos Titel- und Rückseite / Photographs Front Page and Back Page
Werner Huthmacher
Sammlung Deutsches Auswandererhaus / Collection German Emigration Center

Druck / Printed by
MüllerDITZEN AG, Bremerhaven

Verlag / Publisher
edition DAH

2., überarbeitete und erweiterte Auflage / 2nd revised and enlarged edition
Bremerhaven 2009

Auflage / Copies printed
10 000

Impressum Deutsches Auswandererhaus
Credits German Emigration Center

Architektur, Konzept, Gestaltung / Architecture, Concept, Design
Studio Andreas Heller, Hamburg

Ein PPP-Projekt des Landes Bremen und der Stadt Bremerhaven. Seit August 2005 privat betrieben von paysage house 1 Gesellschaft für Kultur und Freizeit mbH. / A PPP project sponsored by the State of Bremen and the City of Bremerhaven. Under private management by paysage house 1 Gesellschaft für Kultur und Freizeit mbH since August 2005.

Wir danken ganz herzlich allen Förderern und Freunden unseres Hauses für Ihre Unterstützung und allen Schenkungsgebern, die unsere Sammlung um Objekte Ihrer Auswanderergeschichten bereichert haben. / We wish to thank the supporters and friends of the German Emigration Center for their aid and assistance as well as all those who have so graciously donated personal objects, thus enriching our collection with their personal history of emigration.

Rechtlicher Hinweis / Disclaimer